Danny Boy

A life of Daniel O'Donnell

First published in Great Britain in 1999 by **Chameleon Books**

an imprint of **André Deutsch Ltd**

76 Dean Street

London W1V 5HA

André Deutsch Ltd is a subsidiary of VCI plc

www.vci.co.uk

Design: **Neal Townsend** for **Essential Books**

Picture research: **Emma Blau** for **Essential Books**

The right of Andrew Vaughan to be identified as the author of this work has been asserted by him in accordance with the Copyright, Designs and Patents act 1988

3 5 7 9 10 8 6 4

Printed in Italy by Officine Grafiche DeAgostini

reproduction by Digicol Link London

A catalogue record for this book is available from the British Library

ISBN 0 233 99487 4

Danny Boy

A life of Daniel O'Donnell

Andrew Vaughan

acknowledgements

A special thank you to all the Daniel O'Donnell fans who opened their hearts about their idol. O'Donnell fans really are an incredible bunch of people.

Tony Byworth, country music's Mr Fixit, has been an invaluable source of information, opinion and access over the past ten years, the gestation period for this book.

Thanks to all those who talked about Daniel, especially Wally Whyton, a good man whose sad death last year has left a gap in the music scene which can never be filled.

And finally, many thanks to Mal Peachey, whose help in my overcoming one particular problem during the writing of this book is deeply appreciated.

introduction

irish singer daniel o'donnell is a

pop music phenomenon who exists

in a world a million miles away

from the hubbub of the pop charts

and radio 1, yet his albums and

videos sell by the millions and he

sells more theatre tickets every

year than any other performer in

england or ireland.

Daniel O'Donnell on the quay of his home town Kincasslagh in County Donegal.

In the past three years he's taken his music around the world including Australasia and the United States, where he sold out the prestigious Carnegie Hall in New York.

Daniel O'Donnell's music is a mixture of Irish ballads and contemporary country music, his smooth, crooning voice squeezing every ounce of emotion from sentimental folk tunes to timeless classics. He's a cross between country and western great Jim Reeves and pop legend Cliff Richard. It's clean-cut wholesome entertainment that appeals primarily to an audience who appreciate uplifting, heartfelt music.

I first realized how good Daniel O'Donnell was at a country music festival at Wembley almost ten years ago. Big stars, like those from America, had won great applause but none held the audience quite so firmly as Daniel O'Donnell. He was young but sang with weary maturity and somehow managed to make every one of that 5000-strong crowd feel he was singing directly to them.

And, unlike many pop entertainers, O'Donnell sincerely appreciates his fans and always finds time to thank them for the support they give. Every year he opens his house in Ireland to the fans and they come in their thousands to drink tea with Ireland's favourite matinee idol.

It's been the oft-told rags to riches tale but with some unusual twists and turns. At a time when his generation were latching on to dance music and new wave rock, Daniel O'Donnell refined the whimsy of standards, Irish favourites and country music. The road to success was littered with coincidence and good fortune. By chance a record company boss attended an Irish festival in London and caught part of the Daniel show.

He liked what he saw and signed O'Donnell to his fledgling Ritz Records. The first album, *The Two Sides Of Daniel O'Donnell*, was released and the Anglo-Irish community in England was captivated by the nostalgic timbre of O'Donnell's music. Demand outstripped supply and both Ritz and O'Donnell

'it's clean-cut, wholesome entertainment that appeals primarily to an audience who appreciate uplifting, heartfelt music'

were born. The debut album would sell over a million copies in the first year.

In 1996 I was invited to a Variety Club Of Great Britain luncheon to honour Daniel O'Donnell. My reason for being there was simply that our paths had crossed on many occasions over the years. As a country music critic I had seen Daniel's rise to the top and had become friendly with people in the Ritz organization. I had interviewed Daniel for a variety of publications on several occasions. At the time I was editor of *Country Music International* magazine in London and was asked to say a few words about Daniel's place in the music industry and within the country music world in particular. The short speech was difficult to deliver since every mention of Daniel's name resulted in huge cheers and screams from the assembled fans. Several years ago I had the idea that at some point I'd write a book about Daniel O'Donnell and I kept the notes from that speech. In order to imagine the speech as it happened one lunch time in Birmingham, try screaming every time you read the name Daniel.

'I think I first met Daniel O'Donnell at the Wembley Country Music Festival in 1988. It was very strange because Daniel was still starting out really and he was quite different to the more established country acts on the bill that weekend. What I remember most, however, was that everyone wanted to

know about this Irish singer. The press were intrigued and the audience spent most of their time trying to get to the Ritz booth, either to try to meet Daniel or to buy tapes and CDs.

'We talked a little then and I couldn't work out how someone so unassuming off stage could become such a larger than life character during his show.

'I remember that at the time I was in my early twenties, as was Daniel, and you really couldn't tell your friends that you liked country music, let alone that you had seen a Daniel O'Donnell concert. In actual fact I'd seen one of his shows a couple of years before in Norwich, but I kept that to myself.

here's to you, daniel

Interviewing Daniel O'Donnell is not a difficult task. He's never less than polite and courteous but one always feels intrusive. Daniel is uncomfortable talking about himself and doesn't like to analyze his career and life too closely. As with all private and public figures, it's often the impressions of others that tell the real story. So significant has been Daniel's involvement in Irish pop music and country music over the past decade or so that, for various purposes, over the years I have asked different people for their impressions and thoughts about Daniel, the man and the artist. Some of those asked are entertainers like Daniel. Others are industry figures and some are just people who have stumbled across Daniel in a variety of ways.

'He's an icon in Ireland, really. It's not my personal style of music but anyone would be a fool to ignore the impact he's had in so many ways. He's created interest in Ireland, sold theatre tickets and millions of CDs and put Donegal right on the map. And all the time he has conducted himself very properly. Good luck to him.'

Susan McCann – Irish country singer

'But at the end of the day Daniel has proved that you don't have to be outrageous to sell records and there's nothing wrong with treating people decently.

'I've been fortunate enough to meet a number of pop legends and a lot of country music stars and most of them have one thing in common. They are not who they claim to be. Very few artists really are the same person off stage as on and the only truly accurate thing I can say to you about Daniel is that he really is everything you always thought he was.'

This book is an attempt to tell Daniel O'Donnell's story in the context of his rise to fame. For an in-depth account of his personal life you should go no further than *Follow Your Dream* (O'Brien Press), written by Daniel with the assistance of journalist and Daniel O'Donnell authority Eddie Rowley.

I have endeavoured to place Daniel O'Donnell within the changing pop culture of the 1980s and 1990s and to chart his career path through the Irish music scene to successful forays in the country music industry and eventually his discovery of a unique style place in the entertainment world in Ireland, the United Kingdom, the United States and Australia.

In researching the Daniel O'Donnell story and sorting through my own files, it became very apparent that the best route to the essence of what makes Daniel such a fascinating character is through those around him. Daniel is uneasy talking about himself but the impact he has had on the lives and careers of many others begins to tell the whole story.

No writer worth his salt should accept any artist's public image at face value and, while this book is a positive account of Donegal's best known pop star, that's not to say that difficult and probing questions were not asked of those who have known and worked with Daniel. The overriding message, however, and one that happily concurs with my own experience, is that he is indeed a gracious and caring person who, as will become clear, has given a great deal of himself to follow his own dream. ❧

Danny Boy

In 1998 Daniel O'Donnell travelled the world, from Chicago to London, Dublin, St Louis and Sydney, but he's still the boy from Donegal and he returns to Ireland as often as possible and still has a home in Kincasslagh, the village where he grew up in the 1960s.

Home by the sea in Kincasslagh, County Donegal.

County Donegal lies in the far northwest of Ireland, where the countryside is wild and rugged. The cliffs are dramatic and the land filled with peat bogs. The beaches are white and often windswept and the whole area feels lonely and remote, a million miles from the twentieth century.

Everyday life for many is hard and, as in so many rural communities, entertainment tends to focus on music. Donegal has thrown up several well-known artists in recent years.

The million-selling new age meets traditional acts Clannad, Enya and Altan all hail from Donegal. Indeed, the resident host at village hall dances attended by the short-trousered Daniel was one Rose Maire Brenna, an aunt to members of Clannad and Enya. Guitar legend Rory Gallagher came from a small village in the south of the county, not to mention many local traditional session players who may not be household names but keep the folk music traditions alive in the numerous pubs and clubs in the hamlets of County Donegal. On a tenuous and quite bizarre note , rumour has it that rock's most notorious bad girl, Courtney Love, scattered her husband Kurt Cobain's ashes somewhere in County Donegal after coming to find the mythical Cobain Nub, a neolithic tomb.

History is still very much alive in this part of the country. The people know and care about the past. History and mythology fuse in an almost surreal fashion and despite hardships over the past thirty years the people of Donegal have always managed to enjoy the 'craic' (good time), especially if it involves playing music.

Travelling around Donegal is best done by car. Public transport seems to take forever and by the time you approach Kincasslagh, having passed through several tiny fishing communities and found many of the local people speaking Gaelic rather than English, it's most apparent that this is a community far divorced from the stresses and strains of the modern world.

Little has changed on the west coast of Ireland since Daniel O'Donnell was born, the youngest of five children, on 12 December 1961, in Dungloe Hospital. Indeed, little had changed in the post-war years before Daniel's birth.

It's a community that still believes in community spirit. The village store remains the central source for all local news and gossip, and dual carriageways and motorways have yet to plunder the rugged green countryside. Life still revolves around church and pub.

At the end of the twentieth century, Kincasslagh and the surrounding areas provide a heavenly respite from the intrusions of the modern world. If it wasn't for the thousands of intrepid fans who have been making pilgrimages to the birthplace of Daniel O'Donnell since the late 1980s, Kincasslagh would have remained a tiny vestige of a lifestyle that's all but disappeared elsewhere. But Kincasslagh is birthplace and home to one of Ireland's most popular and most famous sons. Like it or not (and very few seem to complain) Kincasslagh may just be the most famous village in Ireland. It's not just the fans who know about the Donegal Mecca as, thanks to countless press inches and radio and TV documentaries or features, the public certainly knows about Daniel O'Donnell and Donegal, even if not the absolute details of tiny Kincasslagh.

Back in the early 1960s, when Daniel was learning his way, Kincasslagh was a tight-knit fishing community that protected its own. Visiting the area now and speaking to Kincasslagh residents about their most famous export, there's a noticeable caution in their reaction. Daniel is one of them. They happily accept the fact that he has made their home part of the tourist map but they're not going to speak about Daniel to anyone with an axe to grind. Overcome the hesitation, however, and Daniel's neighbours are transparently proud of his achievements and the manner in which he has dealt with fame and fortune.

Growing up in Kincasslagh, Daniel O'Donnell's family were known as the Boscos, to distinguish them from the other O'Donnells in the area. Daniel explains, 'I know it sounds strange but there were many families with the same name. There were lots of O'Donnells. Back in history O'Donnell had been the most powerful family in Donegal. So a lot of families would adopt some other name. My brother's name was John Bosco so Bosco kind of stuck. But it wasn't like changing your name, I suppose it was more like a nickname.'

The rural west coast of Ireland seemed to miss any of the prosperity the so-called swinging sixties offered other parts of the country. In England they'd never had it so good, but in Donegal things carried on much as they always had. The Boscos, like most in this fishing community, struggled with poverty. The economy simply could not feed the local residents and a large proportion of men had to travel to find work.

Daniel's parents met while working in a fish canning factory in Scotland before coming to Kincasslagh to raise a family. They did whatever they could to bring up five children but, since work in the area was in short supply, Daniel's father Frankie worked as a migrant labourer to feed and clothe his growing family. He often travelled to Scotland for whatever work was available and sent back the bulk of his meagre pay to the family in Kincasslagh. The lifestyle was harsh and, while there's no definite connection between the hardship and his premature death, surviving became too much for Daniel's father and he passed away aged 49 in August 1968 when Daniel was just six years old.

Talking to London's *City Limits* magazine twenty years after his father's death, Daniel admitted that he had hardly known him. 'He was away most of the time I was young and, of course, he died when I was six. It sounds really sad, I know, but thinking back I had a very happy childhood. I was never aware of any insecurities or of ever really wanting for anything. City kids only had a playground, we had the world. The whole world. At least, that's how it felt, with the beach and the hills and all. My mother was extraordinary, she kept everything together. But I still love Kincasslagh. I know times were hard,

here's to you, Daniel

'*It's very interesting to me. I guess we started out at around the same time and over the years a lot of journalists have told me about the incredible popularity of Daniel in Ireland. My own career has been pretty much a rocket ride so in many ways I can understand how Daniel must feel being the centre of such attention. Irish fans love music and the fact they adore O'Donnell says it all, really. I've always believed in treating audiences with the utmost respect and from what I hear Daniel has taken the same belief. I don't know too much about his music but anyone who can sell the number of records he does has to be at the top of the tree.*'

Garth Brooks – country music artist

and they still are, but the people have a great spirit. If you're not used to the country it can seem cold, windy, wet and very bleak but when it's in your blood and you understand how things are it becomes a cornerstone. It will always be my home no matter where I may live.'

In his own book, *Follow Your Dream*, Daniel pays tribute to the way his mother dealt with such a family tragedy.

'It must have been a great struggle for her, because my father never earned enough money to put by savings for a rainy day. So I don't think she had anything at all when he died. Whatever the widows pension was – and it wasn't a lot – she paid the bills out of it.'

For the first five years of Daniel's life, home was pretty basic. The family lived in a small, two-storey house, with life revolving around the fireplace which provided heat, hot water and hot food.

Water came from the well across the street and the toilet was a tin shack across the way. Just before his father's death, however, fortune shone on the Boscos and Daniel and his family moved into a modern council house courtesy of Donegal County Council. The water was laid on and the toilet was indoors – luxury.

The young Daniel's childhood was pretty typical for the time and place: pets, cowboys and Indians in the woods, school, church and occasional treats such as trips to the cinema in Donegal.

Given the financial constrictions of the O'Donnell family, Daniel started work at the tender age of nine years, sweeping the floor and doing general errands in the village's general store, the Cope. Track down the location of the Cope and you'll discover that, not surprisingly, they still remember the young Daniel. And, like everyone in Kincasslagh, they're incredibly protective of him. He's a local hero and his neighbours are very sensitive to the criticism that Daniel has endured over the years. But once it's clear you're a fan (and who else but a genuine fan would know about

Kincasslagh?) they'll tell you that he was polite, very well-mannered and a joy to have around. Anybody in the village who knew Daniel as a child will tell you that he was quiet and hasn't changed at all. A bit like Kincasslagh itself.

From an early age it was clear that Daniel was not cut out to be a manual labourer. He had very little aptitude for working with his hands. Fortunately, he shone in other areas, namely schoolwork and, not surprisingly, singing.

Daniel was something of a loner and didn't fit easily into the rough and tumble games that most of the local boys enjoyed. He preferred the company of girls and despite being picked on by the other boys refused to conform to what was expected. He states slightly bitterly in *Follow Your Dream* that, 'I used to get a lot of slagging. I was soft and they gave me a hard time. They called me a sissy because I'd get up to let some old person have a seat on the bus. And I would never stand up for myself. I'd run a mile rather than fight. I hated swearing and I never used swear words.'

Then as now, Daniel O'Donnell was different. He refused to follow the trends, clearly instilled with a strong sense of identity even from a young age. No wonder the criticism from the self-consciously hip music press over the years that O'Donnell is sugary sweet and too good to be true leaves him simply shrugging his shoulders. He told me in 1988, 'I've always been criticized for being different. Sometimes it hurt, I admit, but I've only ever been who I was and done things that I thought were right.'

Growing up in a predominantly female environment certainly seems to have brought out the sensitive side of the young Daniel O'Donnell. As a six year old without a father he naturally spent most of his time with his mother. 'I suppose you could say that I had no male role model after my father died, because my eldest brother was thirteen years older and my next one four years older and he went away very young to train as a chef... but that's the sort of thing that other people comment on. It's not what you notice at the time.'

As he grew up Daniel become particularly attached to his older sister

Daniel was something of a loner and didn't fit easily into the rough and tumble games that most of the local boys enjoyed.

Margo. Ten years older than Daniel, she was his initial inspiration to take music seriously. Margo started singing in a band when she was just twelve years old and by the late 1960s was having hit records in Ireland. Daniel told *Country Music International* magazine that it was Margo who first turned him on to the joys of country music. 'I grew up with Irish music. My sister has been singing for a very long time, so I was very aware of music in general, especially country music, because she had all the albums and tapes.'

Traditional Irish and country music sit together remarkably well in Ireland. Critics have, in fact, often labelled Daniel's music a hybrid of the two, dubbing his style Country and Irish. Given that so many of the original settlers in America were Irish immigrants, it's hardly surprising that Irish folk tunes became a bedrock for what would develop into modern country music. American country musicians are often surprised to discover that tunes they know by one name are in fact Irish traditional tunes brought over by the original settlers and renamed over the generations. At the same time, because Irish audiences are so familiar with the traditional sound the remaining folk content in much of the best American country music fits neatly alongside their homegrown tastes. That Ireland should develop its own hybrid of the two which would suit the conditions and the culture of the time is no real surprise. Margo was one of the first big stars of this particular hybrid and Daniel, consciously or not, certainly took note.

Margo had started out with her own band The Keynotes in 1964 and by 1968 had hits with 'Bonny Irish Boy' and 'Road By The River'. She appeared regularly on all the major Irish TV shows and by 1972 was a big enough name to grace the International Country Music Festival at Wembley in England. A car accident curtailed her career in the early 1970s, but she recovered well enough to play shows around the world, including Carnegie Hall in New York and the Royal Albert Hall in London. She also enjoyed a long run on TV in Ireland with her own RTE series. Later, as her younger brother eclipsed his sister in commercial terms, her career would include several partnerships with Daniel. A nice reminder of the days when she allowed him to step on stage and pretend to play guitar with her band. She once said that the way to keep ahead of the game was to 'keep your head very level and stay away from the drink at all costs'. Certainly, her brother has followed that advice perfectly. Sadly, Margo has been seriously unwell of late, though she did manage to do some recording with Dolly Parton in 1998.

After Daniel's initial success, there were reports of a certain uneasiness between him and Margo. I remember running into Margo at that time and hesitantly asking her about her younger rival. Naturally, she didn't see it that way and wondered why on Earth anybody would suggest she was anything but pleased for Daniel. She appeared completely at ease with his success. In fact, she seemed like the typical proud big sister.

Despite his lack of manual labour skills, the teenage Daniel took a number of menial jobs to keep money in his pocket and food on the family table, including digging drains and tending a graveyard. And while he never actually dug a grave, he remembers thinking that if digging graves was good enough for Rod Stewart, then it was good enough for him.

After receiving his secondary school Leaving Certificate, he graduated to washing dishes in Dublin's Central Hotel. The job may not have been ideal but it was a stop gap and living in Dublin opened Daniel to the pleasures of

Doing what he does best – Daniel on stage, enchanting the fans.

music on a scale he couldn't have imagined in Donegal. Compared to Kincasslagh and Donegal town, Dublin must have seemed like London, New York and Paris all rolled into one. In the late 1970s and early 1980s it was a thriving hot-bed of live music of different styles. He was out most nights at the Lerne, the National and the Olympic, listening to the big performers of the day; Larry Cunningham, Philomena Begley and, of course, big sister Margo. Partly due to his sister's success and also due to his own personal taste, Daniel's musical persuasion took him towards the peculiarly Irish blend of traditional Irish music and country music. Ireland in the 1960s and 1970s was famous for its showbands. Compared to the cutting-edge sounds coming from the rock circuit across in the UK, Ireland remained the home of the showband. Certainly, folk and traditional music also thrived, but the mainstream revolved around a more cabaret approach. The singers and musicians performed in glitzy sub-Vegas outfits and the music aimed for a middle-of-the-road family sound, mixing in old standards like 'Galway Bay' with pop hits and country music classics. The recording studios at the time

were also geared toward these incredibly popular kinds of acts. Rock acts like Thin Lizzy were forced to move to London to pursue their dreams and it wasn't until 1976, when bands like Bob Geldof's Boomtown Rats appeared, that Dublin spawned its own self-contained rock music scene.

Daniel's musical education had been church and showbands, so his taste and personality fitted the gentle, mellow, easy-going approach rather than the more raucous new sounds coming from Geldof or indeed the high energy disco music that was also transforming the music scene in Dublin. Not only was Daniel more at home seeing shows by the like of Philomena Begley and Ray Lynam, but he totally rejected the nightclub scene, opting instead for the more polite pleasures of ballroom dancing. He was out most nights, usually at the Irish Club, where they specialized in Daniel's favourite dances, the jive and the quickstep. Even now Daniel O'Donnell regularly slips away from his busy schedule to attend traditional style dances wherever he can find them. Pop into Barry's in Dublin sometime and you may well see Daniel O'Donnell doing his own version of the ballroom blitz.

It was fun in Dublin but education was still a priority and in September 1980 Daniel headed west to Galway to begin his studies at the Regional College. Without the excitement of Dublin's nightlife Galway had little to offer. Daniel was homesick and went back to Kincasslagh as often as he could. The journey was tortuous and involved taking a bus to Donegal and then hitchhiking over forty miles to his home. By Christmas break he'd had enough. He told his sister Margo that all he wanted to do was be a singer. Daniel knew many of the performers on the country and Irish circuit and his own sister was a big star. His time in Dublin had shown him the excitement of concerts and live music and the choice between pursuing some white-collar profession or going on the road with a band was becoming easier to make all the time. He spoke to everyone he knew in the music business, asking for advice. Aware of the ups and downs of life on the stage, Margo tried to make Daniel think seriously about it. Her own career had had its high spots and lows and her battle with alcohol had definitely made her cautious of immediately encouraging her young brother into the world of showbusiness. However, she also understood the drive that Daniel showed when it came to performing and finally she let him join her band as rhythm guitarist. Daniel still had to persuade his mother that he should trade a possible career as a teacher for a life in the precarious world of entertainment.

'My sister helped a lot on that side. She made music seem quite a normal thing to do and because she was so successful my mother didn't worry about me going into the same job. Anyway, I'd have hated to get to whatever age and found myself wondering what might have been if only I'd taken the risk with music.'

here's to you, daniel

' *I watched his career build and build and build. You know how the press are, they love to build someone up only to knock them down and several people have tried to knock Daniel O'Donnell over the years. And it hasn't worked. This may sound naive but you really won't find anybody with a bad word to say about the man. You might not like his music but as an entertainer he's in a class of his own and as a person I believe he's as honest and genuine as people will tell you he is. I've interviewed Daniel many times and he's always been very helpful, very cooperative and a pleasure to work with.* '

Howard Dee – Irish country music consultant and DJ

Daniel's debut gig with sister Margo's band was 28 January 1981 at The Rag in Thurles, County Tipperary. It was hardly an auspicious start, since Daniel, being unable to actually play the guitar, mimed his way through the set with his guitar safely unplugged. Eventually, Daniel was allowed to do what he wanted and sing on stage, with Margo giving him seven or eight songs per show. He was learning his craft, watching the audience, observing his sister and filing away every move, every piece of stage work, for later use.

'I was very much a beginner, of course, but my time playing shows with my sister showed me that this was what I really wanted to do. It was wonderful that Margo and I got to sing together and I enjoyed the travelling and the atmosphere and I especially found being on stage thrilling. I never really had any doubts but any that I did disappeared during that time.' Two years after his debut with Margo, Daniel O'Donnell became a solo act. He was finally on his way. 🍃

putting on the ritz

today, daniel's fans are

accustomed to the polished

recordings in their collections and

fond of watching daniel play plush

theatres around the globe,

but the showbusiness world he

entered in 1983 was far

from glamorous.

Far from the bright lights, Daniel takes a solitary stroll by the sea.

On 9 February 1983, Daniel O'Donnell entered Big Tom's studios in Castleblaney, County Monaghan, with around £1000 in his pocket. For £600 he recorded a four-track tape containing 'My Donegal Shore', 'Stand Beside Me', 'London Leaves' and 'Married By The Bible'. For another £600 he put two of those tracks, 'My Donegal Shore' and 'Stand Beside Me', on to a 45rpm single. Initially, he sold the single to friends and family. He even carried a bag of records with him on a bus trip and after breaking into song on the upper deck went round the passengers offering them his new recording. But this was hardly the way to enter the cut-throat world of the music business. With record in hand he was ready to play his music live. His first stop was a trip to friends in Scotland where he sang at Glasgow's Claddagh Club, Irish Centre and Squirrel Club. The response was good. The club owners liked the personable young Irishman and invited him back without hesitation. Now he needed his own band. It was Daniel O'Donnell and Country Fever featuring Peter Healy, Dim Breslin and Joe Rogers. Their first dates were booked primarily in Irish venues in Scotland and England. The English connection eventually proved a masterstroke or a slice of good fortune. Strangely, at the beginning of his career, Daniel O'Donnell found far more success in Scotland and England than he did in his native Ireland. The fact that he had contacts in those countries was a major factor, but so too was his choice of material. Anyone away from their home country and removed from their roots would be more likely to clutch at Daniel's brand of unashamed Irish nostalgia with both hands. In Ireland, while he was following a long tradition of showband-style acts and had learned from his sister Margo, the style Daniel was developing wasn't quite what was played in the clubs in Ireland. What it proved most importantly, a lesson Daniel learned very quickly, was that hard work and constant touring in whatever territory you might choose is the only sure-fire way of building a following.

Daniel was making quite a name for himself in London. North London, home to a great many Irish and London Irish, was filled with pubs and clubs playing country, Irish and showband music. From 1984 to 1985, Daniel and his band were selling out venues like the National in Kilburn. It was already clear that the man had something special.

Irish club DJ and journalist CD Mac, a die-hard country music fan and not one to readily warm to the more middle-of-the-road tones of country and Irish, remembers that Daniel had London fans eating out of his hands in the mid 1980s. 'It was difficult to spot what it was immediately. The material was much the same as plenty of other acts. He could sing pretty well but I think it was something about his presence on stage that made him stand out. Without being disrespectful, many of the acts playing the country and Irish showband kind of circuit were past their best. They might have had some hits back in the sixties but most were just trying to make a living. Suddenly there was this guy in the his early twenties doing the same kind of material but better and with more drive and definitely more panache. He seemed to love performing. He was totally at ease, even in the early days, and he had that eye contact that I think made him a star. I wasn't really involved enough in that particular scene to know how the more established artists reacted to Daniel, but I should imagine that some of the more mature acts were probably a little peeved at his rapid acceptance.' The music industry was quick to spot a potential star. As fate would have it Bill Delaney, of I and B Records, tipped off a record company boss who would prove to be the man to guide Daniel to the very top. Mick Clerkin ran Ritz Records, then a small but very successful independent label, selling bucketloads of albums for Irish music stalwarts Foster and Allen and the Fureys. Clerkin witnessed the O'Donnell charm at the 1985 Irish Festival in London and offered Daniel a record deal.

Mick Clerkin knew the record business. He had excellent connections in Ireland and ran his record company with integrity and a handshake. Ritz then was still a compact family-run operation and Daniel slotted in perfectly. They fitted each other like well-worn gloves. Daniel O'Donnell needed a cosy family set-up around him while Mick Clerkin had an almost evangelical belief that easy listening or middle-of-the-road music had a future. In the bar of the Wembley Hilton in 1988, just after Daniel's inspiring set, Mick Clerkin told me of his belief that not just glory-seeking adolescent pop stars sold records. There was nothing wrong , he believed, with middle-of-the-road music, in fact there were probably more people interested in that particular style than the chart music of the time. The problem he had to tackle was how to expose easy listening music to the public when so many programmers and editors in the media felt that MOR would not fit into the image of their own particular format. With an artist like Daniel, Clerkin reasoned that he had found someone with undoubted star potential and stage charisma who could knock down some of those barriers.

Another record label might well have also transformed the novice O'Donnell into a world-beater, but Ritz gave Daniel the personal freedom to develop at his own pace. And most importantly, nobody tried to mould him into something he wasn't. What was unusual about Clerkin's belief in both his marketing theory and in O'Donnell was that, despite having a successful label with artists selling well, he almost immediately made Daniel O'Donnell the priority act on the label. And at this time, Daniel was still very much untried. Could he last the pace? Was his appeal really broad-ranging enough? Did he have the dedication to learn his craft and undertake all that would be involved in becoming a star act?

If Mick Clerkin had any doubts about the answers to those questions he certainly kept them to himself since, from the outset, Daniel felt absolute confidence in his new record label and, whether he was or not, believed that he was a major priority and would benefit from total commitment by everyone at Ritz.

here's to you, Daniel

' *I also remember one show we did, I think it was in Scotland, and there was a bomb scare. We were all concerned and finally got out of the venue to find Daniel singing to the crowd outside. And another story that shows how he is as a person was when we were in Branson and El Tillis was playing a show. We all wanted to go and see him but it was sold out. The next thing you know Daniel has organized tickets for everyone. And everybody respects him, musicians admire him and trust him. He treats his band very well, pays top dollar. He's a prince of a man really.* '

Danny Shearin – one time Daniel band member

To understand the relationship between the head of Ritz Records and his most important signing, it's important to note that Clerkin also came from humble beginnings in Ireland. Like so many of his peers in the 1950s, Clerkin moved to England looking for work, taking whatever jobs came his way, including time in a factory and a stint as a nightclub bouncer.

Back in 1960s Ireland, the young Daniel might well have been listening to Irish singer Larry Cunningham on the radio while Clerkin drove the bus for the Cunningham band. Everyone trusted Clerkin and he eventually became the band's road manager and then manager. He then started a record label,

Release, which, surprise surprise, released Larry Cunningham records. Release Records worked well for a while but eventually faltered and, phoenix-like, turned into Ritz in 1981, based in a bedroom in west London. Clerkin mixed up his roster with Irish acts like the Furey Brothers, Foster and Allen, Philomena Begley, Ray Lynam, Joe Dolan and country stars such as Billie Joe Spears and Charley Pride. It was into this world that the green but determined Daniel O'Donnell first stepped. First, however, Daniel needed a full-time band and Ritz put it together for him.

Irish band Jukebox had just folded and they, along with Daniel cohort Ronnie Kennedy, became the O'Donnell band. They debuted in Brockley, south-east London, on 6 March 1986. The signs were good. Radio in Ireland started playing tracks from Daniel's first Ritz release, *The Two Sides Of Daniel O'Donnell*, and word was out that there was a new star on the horizon. Things were progressing solidly in the UK and, with the booming pirate stations rediscovering the joys of country and Irish again all across Ireland, Daniel was nicely positioned to build his career in both markets simultaneously. Radio broadcaster Howard Dee, who has been involved in the Irish and country music scene since the 1970s, recalls, 'There was quite a feeling in the early- to mid-eighties that Ireland was going to come up with something big – an artist who would do well internationally. Obviously, several rock acts emerged as world-beaters at that time but I don't think anybody expected someone playing country and Irish and with a showband kind of style would develop like he did. Most music industry folk and reporters felt that the cabaret style was going the way of the dodo. Daniel O'Donnell, in fairness, really reinvented that whole genre. He brought a freshness and a vitality and commitment to professionalism that I don't think had been seen before with that style of music. And, to be fair to the acts who came before him, he had a London record label behind him. I mean, his sister Margo was a big act in Ireland. I remember seeing her on magazine covers in the early seventies with Thin Lizzy. That was the level she was at but she didn't have the record business behind her like Daniel did. I think that was a crucial difference and certainly the fact that Daniel was able to work Ireland and England at the same time and had a solid record distribution machine behind him was very significant.'

Daniel continued building his following in the Irish communities of his favourite towns in England and Scotland, but with Ritz carefully plotting behind the scenes there was now a definite plan to broaden his appeal. Could this artist and his kind of music cross over to a mainstream, non-Irish audience? The litmus test came at the Theatre Royal, Norwich. In his book, Daniel talks of his nervousness at being booked into a venue where the promoter Dick Condon warned him that the audience would only be about ten per cent Irish. But Dick Condon, now sadly passed on, was a theatrical visionary. He had already transformed the sleepy Theatre Royal in Norwich into a thriving and varied arts centre by taking risks with his bookings and bringing in as much diversity as he dared. Not only was this a tough concert since so few Irish would be present, but Norwich audiences are famed for their underwhelming response. Most artists who have played the Royal have commented on the muted response, only to be reassured by the venue that it's simply the norm in Norwich. The audience may love an act but the artist is always the last one to know.

I was at that show, a cub reporter looking to place a review of the concert in some local publication. More interested in the ground-breaking bluegrass of Ricky Skaggs than O'Donnell's easy-listening style of country and Irish, I wasn't expecting to stay long. The plan was to get in, watch some of the show, concoct some pithy put-downs and get back to the real mid-1980s music scene.

Outside the theatre, it was obvious there was something going on from the numbers blocking the adjacent car parks and the queue at the box office.

Daniel's appeal is largely that he represents values which are increasingly difficult to find in the modern world

Condon had been proved correct once again and Ritz and Daniel had the affirmative message sent crystal clear that O'Donnell music was for more than just Irish crowds.

The theatre audience was primarily middle-aged but there was a sprinkling of young fans across the stalls. There was an eerie hush of anticipation before O'Donnell appeared on stage. The audience were more familiar with Daniel O'Donnell than anyone had presumed. From the moment he waltzed on stage, before he even uttered a single note, something quite magical occurred. The whole audience turned as one towards the dark-haired young man from Kincasslagh and from that moment he had their utmost attention throughout the two-hour show. There were no on-stage dramatics, no lighting effects, no instrumental wizardry, but from the way Daniel O'Donnell moved effortlessly through a set of standards like 'From A Jack To A King' and 'Dear Old Galway Town' and 'Lovely Rose of Clare' it was apparent even to a cynical novice music critic that this was a very special evening and a very special artist in the making. In a nutshell, Daniel O'Donnell exuded confidence and presence. From that evening onwards, I was steadfast in my view that whether you like Daniel's style or not nobody could question his charismatic star quality.

Since Ritz had some country music artists on their roster and also because Daniel style fitted somewhere between country and Irish, it made great sense for Clerkin to take on the UK's most experienced country music publicist and consultant, Tony Byworth.

Like Clerkin, Byworth had a reputation for honesty and straight talking and as a former editor of the UK's leading country music magazine, *Country Music People*, he had a wealth of contacts in the UK and in Nashville.

'Well, Mick rang me and asked me to get some press for Daniel. I'd known Mick for a long time and had worked with some Ritz acts and I'd always been very involved in the British country music scene and it seemed to me that Daniel was very much part of that world and that there was potential to really build his career. *I Need You* was the first real album that Ritz was able to get behind and that was really the beginning of Daniel's success in Britain.'

In his book, Daniel tells an interesting tale about that album's title track. 'One night we were playing in a venue called The Georgian in Ballina, County Mayo, and Anne, a fan I had known for a long time, came up to me. She started talking about this song from the sixties that her sister liked and she suggested that it would be my type of song. So I asked her to send it on to me. One day it arrived in the post. She had recorded it onto a tape, obviously from an old record because it was quite noisy and crackly. The strange thing about that song is that when I took it down to Ritz in Dublin to suggest recording it Mick Clerkin already had it in his possession. He had picked it from a totally different source during the same period and he was going to suggest it to me as a suitable song.' It appeared that the connection between Mick Clerkin and Daniel O'Donnell was far more fate than coincidence.

The *I Need You* album was the first O'Donnell recording to really establish the style he's set over the years. It was a polished, expensively produced album with a sweet blend of Irish, country and Irish and country tunes. *I Need You*, recorded late in 1986 ,contained 'Sing An Old Irish Song', 'From A Jack To A

King', 'Lovely Rose of Clare', 'Stand Beside Me', 'Irish Eyes', 'Dear Old Galway Town', 'Three Leaf Shamrock', 'Veil Of White Lace', 'Kickin' Each Other's Hearts Around', 'Medals For Mothers', 'Wedding Bells', 'Snowflakes', 'Your Friendly Irish Way', 'Lough Melvin's Rocky Shore' and 'I Love You Because'.

The music had a timeless feel, the lyrics were largely nostalgic and clearly tugged at the heart strings of the Irish community in England and at the same time it was a surprise to hear such standards sung by a man in his early twenties. A contemporary of Bono and The Edge from U2, Daniel totally rejected what modern pop music had to offer, instead rooting his music in some unattainable yesteryear where the postman still rides a bike, where young ladies wear gloves to the theatre and men are divided into gentlemen and bounders. It was as if those buying Daniel's records were heartily reassured that one so young could be such a decent role model.

A music critic, trying to sum up Daniel's unusual attraction, wrote in 1994: 'O'Donnell's appeal is principally to women who have lived hard lives and whose own families have fallen far short of the ideals O'Donnell sings about. Their own sons have spurned maternal influence in matters of dress and grooming. They may have become roguish ne'er do wells, breaking their mother's hearts. Or, worse still, become their father's sons, sullen and unresponsive. Such sons are not like Daniel O'Donnell. Daniel's followers look from their sons to O'Donnell and sigh. And from such menopausal sighings for an impossibly perfect son has been born the real life Daniel O'Donnell.'

Excuse the sardonic tone of the argument and there is a good deal of truth in those opinions. Daniel's appeal is largely that he represents values which are increasingly difficult to find in the modern world. The mid-1980s were a time of uncertainty for many. In the UK, Margaret Thatcher swept to power with a nostalgic evocation of Victorian values. And in the US, Ronald Reagan took a similar slant with his appeal to the moral majority and the rekindling of family values. While there may only be a tenuous link between politics and

Daniel prepares for a live television appearance on the Gay Byrne Show.

music, there's no doubting that the phenomenal success of certain artists and groups is inextricably woven into the cultural climate of the day. Ritz Records, and Tony Byworth in particular, immediately grasped that what Daniel had to offer was this very nostalgic homeliness. They never tried to present Daniel as something he wasn't just to impress the music community. Neither did they avoid the uncool truths that Daniel was a clean-living, non-drinking pop singer who respected women and treated his elders with due courtesy. There was no pretending. *I Need You* was an unashamed statement of stylistic intent and from that point on nothing has dented the O'Donnell image.

That's not to say that everything was plain sailing. Daniel O'Donnell music had a definite and a growing market but the music industry is largely run by hip young things, or those that like to think of themselves as hip young things, and Ritz and Daniel would never fit easily into that environment. Certainly, with a supportive record label behind him there was no need to pander to the mainstream record business but selling records involves several sectors, many of which were averse to the country and Irish sound. Records have to be distributed. Retail outlets, from small corner shop record stores to high-street multiples like WH Smith and Woolworth to specialist music outlets like Tower, Our Price, Virgin and HMV, have to be brought into the record-selling equation. At the time of Daniel's initial breakthrough with Ritz Records, music business veteran Pat Tynan was General Manager of MCA Records in London. Tynan, with Irish roots himself and a love of country music, was pushing hard to break new country artists from the US in the UK. At that time his focus was on Lyle Lovett, Steve Earle and Nanci Griffith, but he clearly understood the problems that Daniel and Mick Clerkin would face. He explained that, while there was no doubt that the easy-listening market was potentially the most successful in terms of sales, it was a problem with image. Record label sales forces didn't warm to presenting what they perceived as middle-aged mums' and dads' music and the retail outlets in turn often ignored the sales potential in return for keeping the store filled to the brim with the latest *Top Of The Pops* hits. The same thing, Tynan explained, occurred with radio and TV exposure. Programmers were at best cautious, at worst loath to programme anything but the coolest sounds of the moment. Daniel O'Donnell had a growing band of fans but the mainstream press were mocking not just of his style but of the whole clean-cut, goody-two-shoes persona. However, despite the obstacles, O'Donnell records were selling fast. There was a simple demand for product from those who were attending the concerts and those picking up the name by word of mouth. It was as if Daniel O'Donnell existed in a music business world outside of the mainstream. From a record company standpoint, there were two areas to attack: the traditional, easy-listening world of Radio 2 and local radio, and, simultaneously, the British country music scene.

Both Ireland and the UK have long had a great affection for country music of all kinds. Back in the 1960s, one-time Beatles promoter Mervyn Conn

here's to you, Daniel

' *Anybody who performs country music in the UK has my respect. It's a very difficult business because the media is so negative to that style of music. Daniel has his own style, I know, but I learned a lot from finding out how he goes about his business. I think he's a pretty good role model for anyone wanting a long career in this business.* '

Sarah Jory – British country singer

came up with a plan to bring country artists from America to England. Initially it was Johnny Cash who introduced the rockabilly beat and hillbilly twang to thousands of British fans. Later, Conn worked with everyone in the business from Waylon Jennings to Willie Nelson. In the 1960s, Britain fell in love with American country singer Jim Reeves. Known affectionately as Gentleman Jim, Reeves was urbane, sophisticated and sang with a warm velvet voice. He was country's Perry Como and enjoyed massive success in the United Kingdom with hits like 'Distant Drums'. The image and the sound were uncannily similar. And Daniel was a Jim Reeves fan. 'I love Jim Reeves. I don't think I ever heard a song of his I didn't like,' he told *Country Music International*. 'I've covered a lot of his recordings. I suppose it's a market that nobody thought was there. I think a lot of people imagined that the fans died with Jim Reeves, you know. That market, that area of country that includes easy listening is very obvious to me.'

Radio stations around Ireland and the UK play country music either on their main playlist or by way of one or two-hour weekly specialist shows. Mervyn Conn's annual Wembley Festival had, by the 1980s, become a major event, televized by BBC TV and showcasing most of the current favourites from the US.

Conn, like others in the country music industry in the UK, was cautious about booking British acts. Most were unable to match the standards of the American originals and those that were, like the Hillsiders and Hickory Lake and Raymond Froggatt, rarely seemed to achieve the same respect, critically and commercially, as their supposedly superior authentic country cousins. A good number of country music fans in the UK are more aficionados of the American lifestyle than true dyed-in-the-wool music fans. Attend any country festival and you'll see countless fans dressed as Jesse James, Davy Crockett and even Sitting Bull on occasion. The Confederate flag flies from numerous camper vans and the fans will literally spend thousands on visiting Nashville and Texas in search of the real America and real country music.

So the idea of marketing Daniel O'Donnell as country was, on the one hand, quite obvious, on the other it was fraught with difficulties. As with any minority music form, those involved tend to become protective, even precious, about their true love. For the fans who loved Jim Reeves back in the 1960s, it was an easy transition to the updated crooning style of Daniel O'Donnell. But for some in the UK country scene, notably DJs and writers, the boy from Donegal had no place whatsoever in country music.

Nobody in the small but vocal country scene in Britain had anything but respect for Tony Byworth. He'd proved himself a champion of the music, capitalizing on the popularity of country rock in the 1970s with his magazine *Country Music People* while never deserting the hardcore roots of country and western, and then as a publicist working with one of the coolest genuine country singers in the game, George Strait from Texas. Without Byworth's credentials, it might have been difficult to get some of the country fraternity to even listen to O'Donnell. But Byworth was committed and through a vast network passed the message that, while Daniel was not necessarily to everyone's liking, there was no doubting his talent nor his popularity. It was a message that would be told and retold over the next ten years. O'Donnell was receiving decent airplay in Ireland and England but his first real dip into the mainstream of country music came with the 1987 Peterborough Festival.

Daniel was promoting his second Ritz album, *Don't Forget To Remember*, which again was largely a country and Irish collection. The album contained songs such as 'I Don't Care', 'Old Love Never Dies', 'I Wonder Where You Are Tonight', 'Don't Be Angry', 'Roses Are Red', 'Before I'm Over You', 'Take Good Care Of Her', 'Pretty Little Girl From Omagh', 'Don't Let Me Cross Over', 'The Good Old Days', 'Pat Murphy's Meadow' and 'I Just Can't Make It On My Own'.

The country press hadn't particularly warmed to the album. At the time, Daniel was even further removed from mainstream Nashville than he would

have been just five years before. In 1986 there was an explosion in new, cutting edge sounds from Music City USA, with artists such as Dwight Yoakam, Nanci Griffith, Ricky Skaggs, Randy Travis and Steve Earle forging new directions for America's vintage style. But, as would become typical, Kincasslagh's favourite son would have the last laugh. The American stars received the expected respect and many played terrific sets. The critics had picked on Nanci Griffith to be the new Emmylou Harris and most eyes were fixed firmly on the delicate young woman from Texas. And then there was the dark horse, Daniel O'Donnell. Almost without a care in the world, he stepped on stage, oblivious to the mutterings in the arena, and proceeded to show everyone in Peterborough how to put on a show and how to make every member of the audience feel like he was singing to them. It was remarkable at that stage in his career. Like a tennis professional trained to concentrate only on the next point instead of thinking ahead and losing focus, Daniel O'Donnell exhibited a facet of his personality which would resurface every time his career took the next step up the ladder. O'Donnell has never been phased by the big stage. He treats every show, whether it's at the historical Grand Ole Opry or New York's Carnegie Hall, as just another Daniel O'Donnell concert. He was already a consummate professional. In an environment where putting on a show – in the old-fashioned sense – is often secondary to the vocal and instrumental talents of the performer and musicians, he stood head and shoulders above the rest of the bill on performance skills at least.

Mick Clerkin, Sean Reilly (Daniel's manager), Paddy McIntire (radio promotions) and Tony Byworth and all the other Ritz associates behind the scenes had found a strategy that worked. They'd never please all the press but despite the critics Daniel started selling records to country music fans. The Irish crowd were still his home fans but slowly and surely country music was taking note. Daniel recalls in *Follow Your Dream* that 'When you're

rolling, everything fits into place. When I was in Inverness, my tour director Eamon Leahy, who has also played a big role in getting my career on the road, came into my dressing room and told me that *I Need You* was going into the British Country Chart at number 14.'

Three months later, *Two Sides Of Daniel O'Donnell* also entered the charts. It was the beginning of an incredible run of chart domination by Daniel that would lead to some controversial developments. Daniel was also building his appeal in Ireland and in August 1987 'Take Good Care Of Her' backed with 'Summertime In Ireland' hit the number one spot on the Irish singles chart. For Daniel it was a breakthrough moment. 'Records are really souvenirs of the concerts for me. I've read about how people like the Beatles loved spending weeks in the studio. I never have. I love to sing but I will always prefer to sing live than on record. But getting a record in the charts is different. That is something very special and that was my first ever number one. It was terrific.'

Ritz released the new album *Don't Forget To Remember* on 31 October 1987 and just seven days later it entered the UK country music chart in pole position. Despite the commercial success, Daniel was still facing reluctance from radio programmers to include his music on their playlists. Colleen Chandler, veteran BBC Radio 2 producer in England, had long been a country music fan and had spent many years working as producer on Wally Whyton's *Country Club* show, which was broadcast nationally every Thursday evening. Chandler told me that 'while there's no doubt that Daniel O'Donnell is popular we feel that many country music fans just don't regard his music as country in the same was that Waylon Jennings or George Strait is country'. It was a dilemma that would never disappear but for the time being Daniel's sales momentum and list of concert dates were growing by the minute.

Easter 1988 saw Daniel appear at British country music's flagship event, Mervyn Conn's International Festival Of Country music at Wembley, north London. Like Peterborough the previous year, the audience was uncertain whether Daniel and his old time Irish tunes and slushy romantic ballads were appropriate and the assembled press would have been delighted to see him fail. The country music press in the UK are a strange group of people. On the one hand, most write and produce radio shows about country for little or no financial rewards and are in many ways completely devoted to their chosen music style. On the other, at the major events like Wembley many liked to carp and criticize, proclaiming over and over that the new artists really weren't in the same class as the legends of the past. Mervyn Conn always provided luxurious press facilities in a backstage area and while all press members had tickets for the concert hall, most preferred to watch the proceedings from the press room complete with TV and bar. Without naming names, several were particularly dismissive of Daniel before his appearance. I was covering the event for rock newspaper the *New Musical Express*. Having already witnessed Daniel confound the critics on several occasions, I left the press area to watch the show from the wings. Again, the O'Donnell magic lifted the audience. He read out dedications, he accepted flowers and chocolates and skipped merrily through a short but wholly impressive set. What the critics were missing was that they were confusing Daniel's old-fashioned stance with the artist himself. Had O'Donnell opted instead for a mainstream pop career, a cabaret one-man show or maybe light opera, he'd have been a star. The music, love it or hate it, is secondary to what makes Daniel O'Donnell a successful artist. The audience is always transfixed. Critics might argue that while Daniel is an excellent artist he has no place within the boundaries of country music. But the history of country has been one of continual debates about whether one particular artist was in fact country. Was John Denver country? Would modern Nashville class Hank Williams Senior as part of their fraternity? While Daniel was bringing his brand of country to the Wembley audience, over in the United States Garth Brooks was preparing his own version of pop-and-rock-laced country. Again, the classification-obsessed members of the country brotherhood would start talking about the good old days when everything was more straightforward. And just as O'Donnell managed in the UK, Brooks went on to not only confound the critics but sell far more records than the more strictly country artists in the US.

After his Wembley set I wandered the halls of the complex asking some fans for reactions to what they had seen. Daniel fans were, not surprisingly, ecstatic, but positive comments from some of the non-aligned stewards threw a more accurate light on the picture. One said he had never heard of

Daniel but he looked like a star. Was he some big name from America? Along the corridor at the Ritz stand, not long after his performance there was a very long line of fans waiting to buy Daniel's records and merchandise. And there was the man himself, dapper in his Man at C&A outfit, signing, laughing, joking and seemingly enjoying chatting with the fans as much as they were thrilled to meet their idol.

Country music artists in Nashville are famed for their 'meet and greets'. Typically, after a show an artist will appear for signings, hellos and brief chats with their fans. It's part of the tradition of country music and part of the deal. Most do it graciously with a smile on their faces but none enjoy it to the degree that Daniel O'Donnell did that day. There really was no barrier between star and audience: he was one of them, the nice young man from down the road who actually enjoys afternoon tea with the family. He asked the old ladies how they were feeling and slipped effortlessly into banter about hip replacements and angina. And they loved him. It was, without sounding pompous, something akin to a religious ritual.

Still the Ritz machine continued to plan ahead. If the press, radio and TV continued to be wary of Daniel something had to be done to bring his music into the open. As fate would have it, Telstar Records, primarily a TV advertising operation, had been watching the O'Donnell rise with interest and approached Mick Clerkin with an idea to put out two O'Donnell albums on the Telstar label, TV advertise them and bypass the usual media landscape.

Tony Byworth recalls that 'it was a great way of getting directly to the kind of people who would like Daniel's music. People who don't go to the the local record shop or who may be intimidated by going into Virgin or HMV.'

Telstar put out *From The Heart* and *Thoughts Of Home* and the plan worked. Sales went through the roof and even after the deal between Telstar and Ritz ended, Daniel had broken through to a new mainstream easy-listening audience. From now on every album would sell in the hundreds of thousands. ❧

here's to you, daniel

' *People have naturally drawn comparisons but I don't think there are too many. Our style is similar, perhaps, but he's a phenomenon and I'm not. Seriously, he's a decent man who has been very unfairly targeted by some people, but he's had the last laugh, as they say. He'll go down in history as a popular music legend, I believe.* '

Dominic Kirwan – Irish singer

take me home, country roads

after his success in ireland and the uk,

daniel o'donnell was ready to crack

the overseas market – america was

the first choice for two main reasons;

there was a large irish community in

several major cities (notably new york

and boston) and there was the

country music business in nashville.

Several generations of O'Donnells have lived, and died, in Kincasslagh.

'an irish guy going over to

record country songs in the

home of country! it was a bit

like taking snow to alaska.'

daniel o'donnell

So Nashville it was. Tony Byworth, who already had a network of contacts in place, remembers, 'I approached Jo Walker, who was then running the Country Music Association in Nashville, to see if we could do something with Daniel at the annual Fan Fair event. Sean Reilly had his own contacts with bookers and promoters outside Nashville and the whole concept of a US trip began to make sense.'

Fan Fair is an intrinsic part of the country music business. For one week in June practically every major label recording artist takes time off their heavy touring schedules to attend Fan Fair. It's held at the Tennessee State Fair Grounds in Nashville, and over a week's period, for the princely sum of around $90, fans get to see pretty much everyone who's active in the business. The record companies put on short concerts showcasing artists on their roster. From 10am to 10pm, you'll see everyone from George Jones to Garth Brooks playing thirty to forty-minute sets. Even more importantly for the fans, the Fairgrounds are turned into a maze of exhibition halls where every artist will have a booth for signing autographs and selling merchandising. The fans will stand in line literally for hours in the baking summer heat for a chance to shake hands with their idols. One year, Garth

Brooks, easily the best known singer in 1990s country music, stood in line signing autographs for 23 hours straight. This was the world Daniel was about to enter.

Fortunately for Ritz and O'Donnell, Byworth knew exactly what to expect at Fan Fair. Daniel had been invited to represent Ireland on the international stage. Most US fans care very little for country music outside of America, indeed many don't care much for country music outside of the south. Daniel's set was good. He sang 'Take Good Care Of Her', 'Don't Let Me Cross Over' and 'Don't Be Angry', backed by the Jordannaires, the legendary vocal group who had recorded for many years with Elvis Presley. There was a decent late morning crowd but something needed to be done to raise the profile. As Daniel finished, Byworth had all the Ritz contingent and everyone else he could get hold of rush the stage and give the impression that this young man from Ireland was the hottest thing since the Beatles. It worked and fans from all over started heading towards Daniel. Once they were near him they were putty in his charming hands as Daniel did what he does best and took time to joke, sign and chat. The chatting went on a little too long, however. Daniel and his entourage had been invited to a Country Music Association luncheon a couple of miles away from the show grounds. It was a prestigious event and all the international artists on the bill were there promptly. Ritz and Byworth arrived fashionably late and, having explained that the fans kept their boy signing, the word quickly spread around Nashville's curious industry figures that maybe there was an international artist in town who could compete with their homegrown stars. That Daniel handled his exposure with accustomed aplomb is only part of the picture. Taking a country artist to the US and expecting Nashville to embrace them is like asking for a miracle. Country music in Nashville is a closed community. Only very recently have artists and record labels begun to plan international tours and record releases on anything but a token or sporadic level. For an artist to be accepted by such an insular world would take more than talent and charm, it would need good fortune and some of those handy coincidences that had smoothed Daniel's path so far.

There was still more to be done on O'Donnell's debut visit to Music City USA and fortune once again looked on kindly as Daniel was offered a priceless spot at the Grand Ole Opry. Daniel has stated that his proudest moment on that first trip to Nashville was performing at the Grand Ole Opry as a guest of George Hamilton IV. The Grand Ole Opry is known as the mother church of country music. It takes place at the Opry House every week throughout the year on Friday and Saturday evenings. The show is broadcast in its entirety by WSM Radio and segments also go out live on TV on the Nashville Network, which is seen in homes across the United States. Even today, the million-dollar artists are still privileged to be made members of the Grand Ole Opry and huge names like Garth Brooks still perform to the small Opry audience whenever they get the opportunity. Backstage at the Opry is like a living museum. Great names from the past wander the corridors waiting their turn to perform. It's incredibly relaxed. The old guard of performers like Porter Waggoner, Jack Greene, Bill Anderson, Charlie Louvin, Skeeter Davis, Little Jimmie Dickens and so on all know each other like family and the atmosphere is as homely and as warm as befits the best traditions of country music.

Before there was Daniel O'Donnell, George Hamilton IV was very much the nice guy of country music. Originally from North Carolina, he struck big in the sixties with 'Abilene' and was one of the first American country artists to take the music around the world, becoming known as the international ambassador for country music. It was fitting, then, that George should present Daniel to the Nashville crowd. George remembers, 'He did very well. It's always difficult playing the Opry for the first time because of what the place means in country music history. It is a very special place and I was

pleased to help out and invite Daniel along. I have no doubt that he's the
kind of artist who can succeed in America, because he understands people.
Country music is about people; always has been, always will be. These days
it's become a very big business run by corporations and some of the modern
artists have lost touch with their roots. But with Daniel it was like watching a
throwback to a time when the audience and the singers were very much the
same kind of people. He's not been to college and trained to be an artist, he
simply performs from the heart and the people love him for that.'

A few days later Daniel played the Summer Lights festival in downtown
Nashville, this time sharing the stage with George Hamilton IV, Lorrie
Morgan and Ricky Skaggs. At the time, Skaggs was flying high in the US
country charts with a brand of contemporary bluegrass-meets-country
music. He recalls that O'Donnell's performance went better than anyone
might have hoped. 'It's never easy playing to a crowd who don't know who
you are. I have been in that position myself when I've played in Europe – it's a
very different situation to playing for your fans and I realized that Daniel was
used to playing to rooms full of devoted fans. But he was fearless and
seemed to be enjoying himself just being there. It looked like he was just

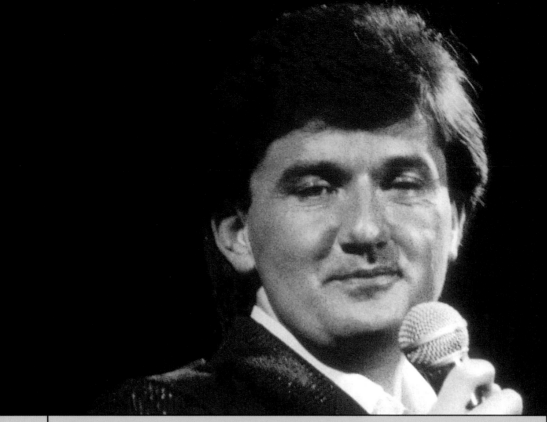

here's to you, daniel

'He did very well when he played for the first time in Nashville. He's a top-notch entertainer. The music is of a particular style that appeals to his audience and he understands how to build an audience over the years. He also has a very attractive persona on stage and it was clear that people in the audience who didn't know him were quite taken by his presence.'

Ricky Skaggs – American country music artist

thrilled to get the opportunity to play in Nashville. He's a real country music fan and that goes a long way in this town, too. His music isn't really what country music is all about here in the US, but I have no doubt that there is a large audience for him and the manner in which he relates to the audience will make him a very big star I'm sure.'

The attempt to create a buzz around Daniel with the influential Country Music Association paid dividends when CMA executive Debbie Brauner moved from the CMA to work at the Nashville Network on the legendary *Ralph Emery Show*. For years, Ralph Emery had been the kingpin of country music television – his show was like the country music equivalent of the *Johnny Carson Tonight Show*. Ritz arranged for Daniel to appear on the show next time Daniel was in Nashville.

It looked as if the plan to break into the country music market was working. For Tony Byworth it was just a matter of doing things the right way: 'I felt it was important that the next step for Daniel was to record in Nashville. Nashville has its own sound and the town has always been hesitant about country music from outside America, in fact Nashville has been reluctant to break artists from outside the traditional country music heartland of the South. To have a chance with radio in the United States we needed an American-produced country album which would be a departure from his previous style.'

Changing the formula for any artist is always a risky business. Daniel's mix of romantic and nostalgic Irish tunes and easy-listening standards had brought him to the surface and the Telstar albums had seen him break into the Top 40 of the British pop charts.

Ritz decided, however, that country music was a very achievable target and that recording in Nashville made a good deal of sense. And as far as Daniel was concerned it was a dream come true. 'Well, I had always been a country fan. I grew up listening to Irish music and country music. I always loved Jim Reeves and my favourite singer is about as country as it gets, Loretta Lynn. She's my favourite singer of all time, male or female. I just think she's terrific.'

Tony Byworth set to work planning Daniel's recording trip to Nashville. Nashville is a small town, a tightknit community that's wary of outsiders, and while there was absolutely nothing wrong with the production and playing on Daniel O'Donnell's previous albums, it made sense to work with a Nashville producer and use the famed Nashville cats on the sessions. Daniel himself prefers to concentrate on his singing rather than getting too involved with the production of his records, so Ritz needed to find someone they could trust and who had a strong name in the Nashville music community. For Byworth, there was one obvious choice for producer

'I had been editor of *Country Music People* in the late 1970s. In about 1977 I'd gone to Nashville to interview Allen Reynolds who had been producing hit records for Don Williams and Crystal Gayle. It turned into a three-day interview and Allen and I became good friends. His work was sympathetic to Daniel's style – it was laid back and easy listening in style. Daniel, in fact, was a big fan of Don Williams and had seen him play in Dublin, I believe, and loved his style. Daniel's style was probably even more laconic than Don Williams and I felt Allen would be the perfect person to understand what Daniel was all about and at the same time make a record that was a genuine country album of the time.'

The first sessions took place in May 1989 at Jack's Tracks on 16th Avenue South in Nashville. The music business in Nashville is particularly unassuming. Jack's Tracks is a nondescript house on one of a small cluster of streets in town known as Music Row. Most of the record companies, recording studios, management offices and publishing offices look more like turn of the century Southern homes than business operations. Daniel himself was nervous of recording with the man who'd been responsible for the success of Don Williams and Crystal Gayle.

taking a country artist to

the us and expecting

nashville to embrace them is

like asking for a miracle.

'I was very apprehensive about going to Nashville to work', he said later. 'An Irish guy going over to record country songs in the home of country! It was a bit like taking snow to Alaska. I had already met Allen Reynolds and I felt comfortable with him. But I didn't know what people would expect of me. How were they going to react to someone coming from Ireland and singing country music in the way that I do?'

But Daniel's trip was very successful. Reynolds immediately understood the style that was needed and had no doubt that Daniel had the vocal skills necessary to make it in mainstream country music. Allen Reynolds used many of the same players who backed Garth Brooks (who he also produced) on his *No Fences* and *Ropin' The Wind* albums and said that 'it was an honour and a pleasure to work with Daniel on this album. I respect him as a professional and am impressed with his sense of songs, his commitment to his audience and his joy in performing. He is also one of the nicest people you could hope to meet.'

Another departure with what would become *The Last Waltz* album was that Ritz decided to avoid the standards and go with original material. Again Byworth was involved in this decision.

'There was a thought that we shouldn't change from what was so successful but it was my belief that the Daniel fans loved Daniel, not just the old songs. They would also love him doing some great contemporary material and at the same time it would give him the chance to be presented as a genuine contemporary act at a time when country music was really blossoming in the US and, indeed, around the world. 'The Last Waltz' was a great song written by Tom Pacheco. 'Marianne' was an old folky song and 'Shelter Of Your Eyes' was a song that Don Williams had found great success with. I think it's a terrific album with very strong material and Daniel sounds totally at ease throughout.'

The 15-song album was scheduled for US release on Capitol, the label that Garth Brooks records for, but unfortunately some political shenanigans at the company left the album unreleased in the US. Its release in the UK and Ireland on Ritz, however, surprised many of the Daniel doubters, such was the quality of the album. Wally Whyton had long been host of Radio 2's *Country Club* show and was a most respected figure in the county and folk world in Europe. 'I wasn't really interested in Daniel O'Donnell's music, to be honest. I thought the fact that he was so popular was interesting and for someone who worked with Cliff Richard back in the fifties I saw some interesting parallels there, but the music really didn't do anything for me at all. *The Last Waltz*, however, is a good record by anybody's standards. The production was very sympathetic to Daniel's voice and I thought he sang the best he ever has on that project.'

The Last Waltz features several Daniel favourites, among them 'Here I Am In Love Again', 'We Could', 'Last Waltz Of The Evening', 'The Shelter Of Your Eyes', 'When We Get Together', 'Ring Of Gold', 'A Fool Such As I', 'Memory Number One', 'Look Both Ways' and 'Marianne'. *Country Music People* magazine voted *Last Waltz* the top album of the year – no mean achievement from a magazine whose readers and critics are among the most knowledgeable country music aficionados in the world.

Another British publication named Daniel the most popular vocalist and Ireland gave him an award as entertainer of the year. With the United States project going ahead slowly but surely, and critical acclaim following behind continued commercial success, it seemed that Daniel O'Donnell was ready for the next big step. Nobody would have imagined that clean-cut, good-living Daniel would be involved in controversy. ✿

chapter

nuns on the Run

Despite the fact that Daniel

O'Donnell has always presented an

immaculate image with no skeletons

in the cupboard, the no-drinking,

no-swearing pop star was about

to, quite unwittingly, be involved

in the most controversial incident

of his career.

Propping up the bar, although Daniel's preferred tipple is tea.

By 1991 Daniel O'Donnell was so popular that he was completely monopolizing the country music charts in the UK. Daniel himself was delighted. An avid chart watcher, it was most satisfying to see his albums taking the top three positions some weeks of the year. The Country Music Association in London, however, felt that Daniel's monopoly of the charts was making the actual chart unrepresentative of what was happening in country music.

Now, this view must be placed in context. The CMA exists to promote the interests of country music. It had been working tirelessly since the mid-1980s to help encourage country sales in the UK and Europe and in particular to explode the myth that country music is a very poor cousin of pop, rock, blues and jazz. At the time it was terribly concerned about the image problem facing country music. Ten years before the likes of Shania Twain and LeAnn Rimes, country was still perceived by the public and the record business as genteel, rather corny old people's music, to be avoided at all costs. Artists like Dwight Yoakam, Steve Earle and Lyle Lovett had recently started to challenge that position and it looked to the CMA that, what with Garth Brooks proving so phenomenally popular in the US, and willing to tour internationally, it was time to clean up the chart, make it as hip and contemporary as possible and try to establish country as cool. That was the plan. Unfortunately, Daniel O'Donnell simply sold more records than anybody else. Byworth remembers : 'I believed that, if the chart is based on sales, then to remove Daniel would be to prejudice the charts. It wasn't the right thing to do.'

However, Daniel was removed from the UK country chart and then the fun started. The Daniel O'Donnell fan machine sprang into action. To the average record buyer, an industry decision like the one to remove him from the charts would appear remote and hardly worth taking an interest in. But once the Daniel O'Donnell fans rallied, their outrage was hard to contain. Letters were fired off constantly to local newspapers, radio stations, the Country Music Association and, most famously, an order of nuns in Ireland wrote, so the story goes, to *The Times* expressing their concern. After that the press picked up on the story and began to write about Daniel for reasons other than his music. This was a story. How could such a decent, personable young man be so shabbily treated by the music business? It was a storm in a teacup, but for the first time Daniel O'Donnell's name was heard outside the country music and easy listening world. What had started as a genuine attempt to limit his control of the charts, in order to help the general sales of country music, ended up looking like a publicity masterstroke by Daniel's people. As Tony Byworth recalls, 'Once the decision was made to go ahead it was down to the fans.'

The fans mounted a very vocal and very forceful campaign and the publicity that came Daniel's way was obviously excellent for his career. The

'they say that there's no such thing as bad publicity, but in the end it was all getting to be a bit too much for me.'

Daniel o'Donnell

knock-on effect was considerable. One of the UK's most important retail outlets, WH Smith, began to discuss the possibility of stocking more Daniel O'Donnell and thinking of ways to utilize the growing exposure as a direct result of the chart debate.

It wasn't a controversy where he'd done something wrong. All Daniel had done was sell more records than anybody else in the chart. For Daniel it was an unpleasant period.

'I was a little embarrassed by all the fuss. They say that there's no such thing as bad publicity, but in the end it was all getting to be a bit too much for me. And when the Country Music Association finally reviewed the situation and decided after four months to reverse their decision, I was more than relieved. I don't know what effect it would have had on my career in the long term if I hadn't been allowed back in to the country chart. But it definitely didn't do me any damage during the short period that it lasted. If anything, it only increased my profile and probably helped to win me a lot more support. I'm very grateful to the fans, the media and everyone who supported me during that saga.' ❧

on the road again

visitors to kincasslagh, unless they are

very well informed, are often

surprised to find that their idol is not

at home — aside from touring ireland

and the uk pretty much constantly

since the mid-1980s, daniel has more

recently pursued america and

australia, and to sell records in a new

territory means touring as often as is

humanly possible.

A windswept walk long Kincasslagh quayside.

In England it all started in a small van; a shoestring operation which saw Daniel driving through the night, week after week, in order to make the shows. 'Oh, it was tough in the beginning. We didn't have enough money to travel in comfort. Sometimes the van would break down, sometimes we didn't have enough money for a motel room. And even though I was always excited about getting to the next show, I was often very tired. Travelling really does take a lot of energy. But I knew, from knowing how the business works, that you have to be out there and you have to play as often as you can. There is no better way to build your career and you know that if you have the talent eventually the discomfort will dwindle and the touring business will become a much more pleasant experience.'

Never mind how ramshackle the travel and accommodation arrangements may have been, the audience would never have known about the mishaps on the road. Even at the outset Daniel was always immaculately turned out on stage and had the utmost respect for the people who paid money to see a show. At the same time, he himself remained at heart a fan for whom the idea of travelling to America and playing shows around the world was more than a dream, it was for so long a fantasy.

In the late 1980s, country music legend Dolly Parton visited London for a few days of promotion and publicity. Tony Byworth was handling the media event and on the morning of Dolly's press conference in a top London hotel he brought Daniel along. Daniel by this time was an established name on the circuit and probably sold as many albums if not more in the UK than Dolly Parton, but he was awed just being in the same room as the Queen Of Country Music. We chatted in the lounge and he seemed to forget that he too was a star of some magnitude. I commented that he must know what it's like to be the centre of attention and to have photographers straining for one more picture, but he couldn't see the connection. This was Dolly Parton, a genuine star in his mind. He wanted her autograph and picture more than anything. Daniel also said that afternoon how impressed he was that Dolly was known throughout the world and that she was able to communicate with people in so many countries.

Maybe that day sowed the seeds of his determination to break through in America and, later, Australia. For many, international success is all about money or pure ego. For Daniel, it really seemed more about being able to meet people from as many different cultures and walks of life as possible. He is undoubtedly a shrewd businessman and has always been noted for his absolute dedication and professionalism to his craft, but the underlying motivation was to relate to more people. It's the magic ingredient of his phenomenal success. Performing to hundreds of new fans in Boston or New York is a thrill, but the real deal for Daniel is actually conversing with the audience, both on stage and off.

A Daniel O'Donnell concert is the complete showbusiness event. A concert in Missouri in the late 1990s showed me just how far he had come from the talented but unpolished performer I first saw in Norwich ten years previously.

Branson is a small town in the American state of Missouri and was built almost exclusively on the tourist business. It's like a cross between Las Vegas and Nashville, with neon and music drawing the traveller into the waiting arms of hundreds of hotels and countless theatres. For a while, Glen Campbell, country star and some time movie actor, had one of the first theatres in Branson. He explains the nature of the city: 'It's a place where you can see some of the older, maybe not so fashionable acts like Andy Williams and Barbara Fairchild and myself. The beauty for the artists is that we can play a summer season and the fans come to us. We don't have to travel. The tourists have nice hotels and there are some beautiful theatres in town.'

Branson doesn't exist at the cutting edge of the music business. It's a place where popular artists who perhaps no longer have a chart presence can still play to adoring crowds. And for an artist like Daniel O'Donnell it's the prefect environment. The audiences remember the legends of entertainment and expect a real show. That's exactly what O'Donnell gives them.

It starts with Daniel waltzing through the audience like the prodigal son coming home to a family reception. He sees fans he knows and stops for a chat, always remembering their names.

Backing singer Danny Shearin noted recently: 'I don't understand how he does it, but once Daniel has met someone he remembers their name and often little details like where they are from. It's not a trick. To me it's a gift he has and I think it's because he actually feels like he's meeting a person, not just a member of the audience.'

Dressed immaculately in three-piece suit and without a hair out of place, Daniel happily poses for pictures and takes note of song requests. Many will indeed feature during the show. Then Daniel disappears, allowing Ritz stablemate Mary Duff to take the stage. Like Daniel, she plays a mixture of standards, Irish songs and country. The audiences at his shows are always very loyal and kind towards Daniel's cohorts, but it's the boy from Donegal they really want to see. The anticipation is quite unnerving before Daniel makes his entrance and launches into a bouncing version of 'Together Again' from his gospel album, *I Believe*. Between songs he jokes with the band, keeping the audience guessing as to which songs he'll perform in this particular show. With so many O'Donnell fans likely to attend more than one show, during a concert stint he has to keep the nightly performances varied. But the concerts take on an almost organic state. He's the star, no doubt, but the content of the show evolves with the interplay of the audience. Depending on the requests and dedications, on any given night he'll pick certain appropriate songs and the audience love him for it. The performance is smooth, the band note perfect is it moves seamlessly through a series of O'Donnell favourites: 'Shades Of Green', 'I'll Take You Home Kathleen', 'Galway Bay' and more. Things get pretty lively when he launches into an

here's to you, daniel

' I know about being teased for being religious and so-called clean-cut, but you have to be true to your beliefs. When I first met him he seemed a very pleasant shy young man and whenever I've run into him over the years he seems exactly the same, which is testimony to himself, his family and those around him. And I do believe that if he keeps touring America he will eventually make a very big name for himself, because his show is quite unique these days. '

George Hamilton IV

Elvis medley, suggesting that Daniel O'Donnell rocks after all. Then follows a spirited audience participation favourite with Roger Miller's timeless 'King Of The Road'.

The success in Branson, as with the rest of his career, has been built slowly from a solid foundation. Daniel remembers his first concert series in Branson: 'It's a terrific challenge. It's something I think I needed more than I realized. When I opened in Branson nobody knew me and it was like starting over again. Sometimes you get to a stage when you think, "Was I really able to do this? Did people really like me?" Everywhere I do shows the audience responds well. People say that I represent a certain feeling for them. I worked in Branson where nobody knew me and I saw people begin to smile, allowing me to enter their lives. I know from speaking with them that, whatever it is that I give them musically and in entertaining, I still have it. The people appreciate it just as they did ten years ago. I felt renewed by the experience. I started the first day with about fifty people in the audience and I finished after the tenth with about four hundred.'

Most interesting is the transformation of Daniel's personality. Off stage he's confident but definitely shy. He's a secure and well-adjusted man but he finds it incredibly difficult to talk about himself. But on stage there's a personality release. He's light-hearted, humorous and grows in stature with every round of applause and every scream of 'Daniel, we love you.'

It's a cliché that so many entertainers, whether comedians, actors or musicians, are insecure and shy away from the glare of the spotlight, but it's also very true in many cases. The most startling example of Daniel's discomfort that I've seen came at a Variety Club luncheon in a swanky hotel in Birmingham in 1996. It was a prestigious and important event. Daniel takes his charity work very seriously. I had been asked to address the audience and speak about the importance of Daniel O'Donnell in the country music industry. Daniel, his entourage and the speakers sat at tables on a stage and the ballroom was filled with industry figures and fans who had paid a good deal of money to be close to him. As a fund-raiser it was a massive success, with tables squeezed into every corner. During the preamble Daniel's body language was such that he was making himself as small as possible. His shoulders were hunched and he sat low in his chair. I swapped a few words but clearly he was feeling awkward at the attention and the importance of the event. He told me that he feels embarrassed being praised and, while many in the audience were fans he recognized, it felt very different to a concert. The function under way, he chatted politely to the local dignitaries waiting for the presentations to begin.

As I addressed those assembled in the ballroom I realized the impact Daniel had on his audiences. My first line was that I had known Daniel for several years, but as soon as I uttered the name 'Daniel' the room went crazy with screaming, cheering and one or two tears. The emotion in the room was almost visible and for those of us without O'Donnell's stage experience quite disconcerting.

Speeches over, and in my case cut short due to stage fright, Daniel Bosco from Kincasslagh did a quick Clark Kent impression and turned dramatically into Daniel O'Donnell, Superstar. He left the formal dining area and bounded through the audience, stopping at tables, signing autographs and grabbing certain ladies from their tables for a quick fandango. It was remarkable. This was his natural environment. Uncomfortable making small talk at a luncheon in his honour, he showed himself instead absolutely at home with his fans.

And that's how it is on the road. Danny Shearin was backup singer with Daniel for about three years. 'He's quiet, I suppose, and he does keep himself to himself. But he's still one of the lads. He likes a joke and a laugh like everyone else. But it is like he's two people, or maybe it's that when he's on stage he just becomes a bigger version of who he is off stage. But he's only so comfortable performing, I think, because he works so hard. He knows exactly what he's doing. He prepares and he plans. He's very professional. And travelling with Daniel is not like travelling with anyone else. I've been around the UK and America with him, and most of the time fans travel as well. Travel companies organize tours to take fans on the Daniel tours so they'll often be in the same hotels. He doesn't lock himself away in the penthouse suite. In fact, I remember one time in America I saw him on the balcony of his room leaning across chatting to a lady fan who was a few rooms down and talking about what colour shirt he should wear and that kind of thing. He's a very normal person and I think he enjoys spending time with the fans as much as he does playing music.

'They say that fans can spot a phoney and you couldn't try to copy what Daniel has done with another artist because you'd have to really be genuine to be able to spend as much time as he does with the people who come to his shows. He's definitely a one-off in my experience.

'I remember at one show in America there was a fan in the audience, she was a 94-year-old lady, and Daniel knew she was there. When he spotted her he went straight up to her on her balcony seat and started to dance with her. It was incredible.'

Folk singer Clive Gregson comes from a very different world from Daniel O'Donnell. He had a short-lived pop career with new wave band Any Trouble in the UK before entering the folk world and becoming something of a cult act with a strong following in Europe and America. And while you'll find critics happy to mock the Daniel style, performers rarely do. 'I saw him a few times in England,' says Gregson. 'A friend of mine promoted some shows in the Midlands. He's good; an excellent performer and anyone who can have that kind of an effect on an audience has my respect.'

But those few hours on stage can only take place thanks to strong organization and a well-oiled machine that manages Daniel's career on the road. Mick Clerkin, of course, started out working as a roadie and knows a thing or two about planning a tour. And Daniel's personal manager Sean Reilly has been a godsend over the years, utilizing his experience on the road to smooth out any problems that might arise. Reilly has worked with Mick Clerkin since the 1960s, beginning as road manager for a band called Gary Street And The Fairways. He progressed to managing legendary Irish country singer Ray Lynam, before taking on Daniel O'Donnell and Mary Duff. Reilly, like everyone else involved in Ritz, is most unassuming and concerned only with ensuring that Daniel's career moves along with as few hiccoughs as possible. It was Reilly's contacts in the Irish venues in America that allowed the first US tour to be so successful.

In 1991, with the *Last Waltz* project out of the way, Daniel again visited the United States. The concerts in the UK and Ireland were consistently selling out but tackling America would involve starting over. Daniel had made something of a splash in the country music world in the US with his first visit in 1988, but to create a mass following around the country he'd have to tour and build up a following as he'd done in the UK five or so years previously.

Building a music career is just like building a house. Once the foundations are in place every new level has to be carefully layered. Without the right structure the roof will fall off! Ritz understood that Daniel would have to start small and build a following, initially by word of mouth. They also needed a solid press campaign. Pam Lewis, Nashville publicist and one time co-manager of Garth Brooks, was recruited to direct Daniel's campaign in the United States. By this time, Garth Brooks was rapidly becoming the most successful artist in country music history, so she was perfectly placed to direct a campaign for an artist who in some ways shared many of the qualities which made Brooks so popular. Like O'Donnell, Brooks took time to treat his fans with respect and thought nothing of devoting hours to interviews and meeting and greeting the fans who paid good money to see him. Pam Lewis recalls that, 'The difficult thing with Daniel was marketing him as country music. In the United States the definition of country was very different to the definition in the UK. In America Daniel is more of an easy-listening artist and country radio would not classify his music as country. So we had to find another way of promoting Daniel. Obviously the Irish community in the north east was a good place to start.'

With a ready-made market, Daniel began by playing small Irish venues in Boston and the north east. It worked. And the size of the venues steadily grew until he was able to sell out the most prestigious concert venue in the United States, Carnegie Hall. On 22 May 1991, Daniel O'Donnell's name went up in lights outside Carnegie Hall. The show was a sell out. Daniel recalls the event in his book.

'I got a bit emotional when I went out on to the stage that night for some strange reason. I recall how I told the audience, "I never thought I'd get the opportunity to say this: Welcome to Carnegie Hall." Then I went straight into a song because I felt I was going to break down. I never thought I'd see the day when that would happen to me. A flood of emotions hit me. I think what happened to me was a result of seeing a number of people I knew, sitting in the front row. I remember asking myself "How did I get here?"'

After several forays into the American market, with venues and audiences growing every visit and Daniel's albums selling well on import, it was time to look at another foreign market, Australia. As with America, Australia has a strong Irish community and a growing country music industry.

Again it was Tony Byworth who worked behind the scenes plotting Daniel's recording career and visits to Australia. 'I first spoke to a guy in Australia called Laurie Dunn in about 1992. He was interested in Daniel but nothing came of the conversation. In 1993, he was working as Managing Director of Virgin Records in Australia and we met in London to discuss Virgin releasing Daniel's albums in Australia. Mick Clerkin and myself had been to Australia in 1988 or '89 and it was an obvious market. There was a vast Irish

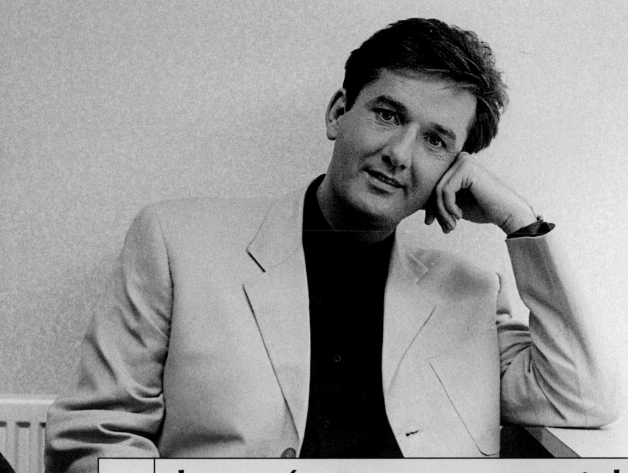

here's to you, Daniel

' He's an icon in Ireland, really. It's not my

style of music but anyone would be a fool to

ignore the impact he's had in so many ways.

He's created interest in Ireland itself, sold

theatre tickets and millions of CDs and put

Donegal right on the map. And all the time he

has conducted himself very properly.

Good luck to him. '

Tom Gilmore – country music DJ, Galway, Ireland

community and Mick had some success already with the Fureys and Foster and Allen. Well, when EMI bought Virgin, Laurie Dunn left the company but he soon started his own operation, Massive, and he signed Charley Pride and Daniel O'Donnell to his Australian operation.'

By the end of 1998, Daniel had made five Australian tours and, as with his forays into England and the United States previously, finished up playing the most prestigious of venues; the Sydney Opera House. Australian fans are now part of the growing international community of O'Donnell aficionados, and at the time of writing Daniel has just finished his most commercially successful tour Down Under so far. The country music community has taken warmly to Daniel in Australia. Since the days of legendary Aussie cowboy star Slim Dusty, country music has been a staple of the musical diet in the South Pacific. Indeed, Nashville's most successful female artist of the past ten years, Reba McEntire, recently played to sell-out crowds in Melbourne and Sydney. Nashville's *CMT* (Country Music Television), after failing to draw enough viewers for its European service, is finding very promising ratings in Australia. For an artist like O'Donnell, adept at both country and a more traditional Irish format, his chances of real success are very strong.

The situation in the United States improved dramatically in 1997 when Ritz struck a deal with Honest Entertainment to sell Daniel's music in the States with three repackaged albums comprising songs taken from existing albums. The three albums, *This Is Daniel O'Donnell*, *Country Collection* and *Irish Collection*, showcase songs from Daniel's previous Ritz albums. Crucially, Ritz would no longer have to rely on importing records into the US and finding distribution as outsiders. The deal with Honest meant that Daniel O'Donnell albums received a proper American release and could begin to fight the sales battle on an equal footing to American artists. And if anyone doubted the potential demand, an appearance by Daniel on shopping channel PVC on St Patrick's Day 1998 saw the entire stock of 3000 albums

sold during the first hour of the show. Daniel had been booked for another appearance, but it had to be postponed until the record labels could get enough CDs into the country to satisfy the demand.

Veteran music critic John Lomax, who manages an Australian country band and has written extensively on the Nashville scene for several years, says: 'I don't know if he'll ever be accepted by country radio. That's a very difficult situation, even for people like George Jones and Dolly Parton right now. But I have no doubt that if Ritz, Honest and Massive are able to market Daniel in creative ways, then his audience and record sales will simply increase. He has everything it takes to be an international star.'

chapter

everything stops for tea

in 1989, daniel o'donnell was chosen

as donegal person of the year — the

accompanying citation is testament

to the very special relationship

daniel enjoys with his fans.

Old haunts. Daniel visits the shop where he got his first job.

Daniel never forgets those who put him where he is today.

'Daniel O'Donnell is a perfect example to the youth of our county and country. Success has not gone to his head. He has never forgotten his roots. He has not forgotten his mother and his family. He has not forgotten his beloved Kincasslagh and Donegal. And, above all, he has not forgotten the people who have put him where he is today – his loyal fans. He is never too busy to stay behind after shows to talk to them and sign autographs. Many are the stories that could be told of his visits to homes and hospitals to meet sick fans, even when this meant interrupting busy schedules. One story which displays his concern for his fans is the one which tells of an occasion when it came to his notice that some fans, who were itinerants, were being refused admittance to his show. He refused to go on stage until they were admitted. Daniel never loses an opportunity to lend his name and his services, if possible, to worthwhile charities. A non-drinker and non-smoker, his clean-cut image in his dress and in his living standards does not meet with the approval from some gurus of the media who seem to wish he were otherwise. But they meet with the approval of us here in Cumann Tir Chonaill (County Donegal).'

Daniel O'Donnell is as famous for his relationship with his fans as he is for his music. Critics from the mainstream press and the music papers may not find his crooning to their taste but none can ignore the phenomenon of Daniel O'Donnell. So well-known is the spectacle of thousands of largely middle-aged women travelling the country (and often the world) to follow Daniel that a play was even staged in London in 1998 entitled *Women On The Verge Of HRT*. It was a humorous and insightful tale of a group of women getting to know each other on a trip to see their idol, Daniel O'Donnell.

Many tales have already been told throughout the previous chapters of Daniel's devotion to those who pay the bills and his uncanny ability to relate to them all on a personal level. Talking to fans is usually a difficult task. Most pop fans are young and impressionable and many artists attract fans who seem to have lost all sense of reality. Country music, thanks to the surface openness between artist and fan, does attract many who have a very skewed version of reality. In one year I met three different women who claimed to be married to American country singer Dwight Yoakam – who was and still is happily single. But Daniel fans are a different breed. Most are older than the average pop fan and many, certainly the majority, are women. These are people who have lived a little, probably raised a family and are not likely to be duped by a smooth, velvet-voiced pop singer. What they all recognize in Daniel, and what brings them together, is his honesty. Ask every fan about Daniel and after they've talked about the music, the concerts and the humorous incidents, they will all come back to the word 'genuine'. For Daniel O'Donnell fans, his integrity and commitment to being a decent person count more than anything. The fact that he's a delightful singer and showman is essentially the icing on the cake.

A letter from Debbie, a dedicated Texan fan, illustrates this perfectly. 'Daniel's so very genuine and special. An e-mail pal's dad was ill in hospital and couldn't attend a concert – Daniel called him up to check on his condition.

'Did you know that Daniel's father was the seventh son of a seventh son and that he was known to have curative powers? I was told that by a Scottish fan this summer. Some believe that Daniel has inherited some of that. I love his calmness. Daniel has such a calming effect on people. I normally get very nervous around performers – don't know why – just do. But with Daniel I always feel that he is just talking to me and no one else.

'Until Daniel came along I was a devoted country music fan. Now all the albums and CDs I've collected over many years (way over 500) pretty much are collecting dust because they just don't compare to Daniel.

'I first met Daniel in June 1997 in Branson, Missouri. I had seen a very brief news clip on TNN stating that Daniel enjoyed the same level of success in Ireland that Garth Brooks enjoys in the USA. I remember that I didn't pay much attention to the clip. Then, when I made my yearly trip to Branson, who was playing at the Barbara Fairchild Theatre but Daniel O'Donnell? I told my husband and my daughter, "We're buying tickets and we're going".

'So here we walk in the theatre and there stands Daniel behind the concession counter, trying to figure out just how southern folk are going to react to him. I didn't know until later that this walkabout is what Daniel always does before a show. This day he just landed at the concession counter to sign a few autographs before the show.

'Daniel is having problems with our southern drawl and we're having trouble with his Irish. He laughingly tells us that if we each repeat it enough times the meaning will eventually become clear. He is very kind to a child with a serious illness and he asks for a hug. Then and there I saw in Daniel a true, genuine person, before I had even sat down in my seat for the show. After the first song I was in love. I sat there in heaven for the rest of the show. I left determined to learn all I could about Daniel.

'Daniel has something that country music has let go by the wayside. Daniel is the way country music should be and isn't. Daniel is the only

here's to you, Daniel

'*I know I'm not supposed to be a Daniel fan. It should be Boyzone, I suppose, or whatever is in Smash Hits. But I heard Daniel all my life growing up and he feels kind of like part of the family. He's like a big brother who does concerts and you feel proud of him because he's one of us. I think he's very down to earth. I know most of the fans are much older than me but they're a lovely bunch of people mostly. And I don't care what my friends say. I like chart music too, but Daniel will always be number one.*'

Michelle Kinnearey – Irish fan, 22 years of age

performer that I know of who modifies his show to fit requests as much as possible. He did this so much in the three shows that I attended in 1998 that several times the musicians were frantically searching for the music in question because it hadn't been planned. The look on their faces! Daniel told them it was an opportunity to rise to the occasion ,well, if they didn't we would understand that they had tried.'

There are literally thousands of stories about Daniel playing a significant part in ordinary peoples' lives. David from Bromley, England, doesn't like to classify himself as a fan but his letter perfectly typifies the affection in which Daniel is held by many.

'My wife and I attended a concert back in the mid-eighties and she immediately fell for Daniel's charm. The music was very pleasant but we were both struck by Daniel's presence. Never before had I seen such a pleasant performer on stage. The only comparison I could make would be with Cliff Richard – I think they share many of the same qualities. Unfortunately my wife became very ill not long after we saw Daniel in

*. . . above all he has not
forgotten the people who
have put him where he is
today — his loyal fans.*

concert, but I was able to buy several videos and CDs to keep her happy at
what was a very difficult time. I really didn't understand how things worked
with record companies and managers and things like that, but when my wife
became very sick I wrote to the address on the back of a record asking if they
had information of any concerts coming soon because I really wanted to let
my wife see him again before it was too late. I suppose that in my very
emotional and upset state I probably said something about her having a
terminal illness, not something I should have done, perhaps, but the people
there were so nice that they sent me a package of Daniel records and videos
and said my wife and myself could meet Daniel at a show very soon. It was a
marvellous gesture and I realize from finding out more about Daniel since my
wife passed away that it was a genuine offer. Sadly, she died before we could
meet him, but I can assure you that his kindness and the courtesy of the
people at Ritz Records made a lasting impression on my wife and myself.
Isn't it a strange world we live in when people are suspicious of people who
do good deeds? I have read articles about Daniel where the writer seems to

want to discover that it's a big confidence trick. As far as I'm concerned that's very tasteless and people ought to know that Daniel O'Donnell is exactly what he says he is – a straightforward and decent man.'

Fans throughout the world echo these sentiments and, through the mail and increasingly through e-mail, many have become friends through Daniel O'Donnell. It's a tight and protective community with perhaps a little friendly rivalry over who has seen more shows or who has the best collection of souvenirs. But it's harmless fun. And for most the ultimate moment in any fan's Daniel career is making that pilgrimage to his open day in Kincasslagh, County Donegal.

Over the years, since his early days trekking around the country, Daniel would invite fans to visit him for a cup of tea the next time they were in Kincasslagh. It started out as a light-hearted comment but fans (being fans) started taking him up on his hospitable offer. With videos for sale that were often filmed in his home town, the fans already had an idea of where their idol was from and the logical next step was to actually visit. Often fans would find the house but no Daniel, such was his touring schedule, but they were always greeted kindly by his family. But with the number of visitors growing, Daniel hit upon the idea to get this tea business organized. He was nearly always at home in the summer for the Mary From Dungloe Festival in Dungloe. He told fans about the festival and picked a day in July when they should come and visit. In 1992 almost 3000 people queued for hours to meet their hero.

The tea party in 1998 had to be the last for a few years, however, thanks mainly to his increased workload and commitment to touring the US and Australia and possibly South Africa. It was a very special day and over 7000 turned up to meet Daniel. The event has become so enormous that an airport eight miles from Kincasslagh, at Carrickfin, had to be built to help cope with the number who turn up for this event and at other times during the year.

The fans' special day is like a cross between a church fete and a

Back at base. Relaxation for the wandering star at last.

pilgrimage to Lourdes. The rain is pouring and the whole area is swarming with fans, heads bowed from the rain and treading the winding lanes towards Daniel's bungalow on the edge of Kincasslagh. With so many in attendance they'll only get a fleeting moment with Daniel, but it's well worth the wait and the journey. As the line shortens they get closer to meeting the man himself and having their picture taken with Daniel by his sister Kathleen before moving along for a nice cup of tea and a certificate saying they have met the great one. The smiles on the faces prove that, despite the typically poor weather and the sheer volume of the event, nobody feels cheated by such a brief chat with Daniel. They completely understand the situation.

But for the lucky ones there's more to come. Advance planning has resulted in some staying in the 15-room Viking House Hotel, in Kincasslagh, which is owned by Daniel, and the chances are that their host will pop in later for a game of cards and another nice cup of tea.

Although the vast open day has been postponed for a while, fans still get to meet Daniel at his home town at other times of the year. Ann from Newcastle met him in 1998 on one such trip.

'We met Daniel in June this year. Neil (my husband) and I went on a

here's to you, Daniel

'*He was always a very pleasant young man. I don't think he's ever really grasped just how important he has been in Irish music. He'll continue to become more popular and a better artist as time goes by. I worked with Cliff Richard many years ago and there are many parallels. Like Cliff, Daniel has managed to become famous without any scandal or outrage or simple unpleasant behaviour to get his name in the papers.*'

Wally Whyton – broadcaster (now sadly passed on)

Donegal tour which is organized by the Viking House Hotel – so that you actually meet Daniel while you are there. I was a bit worried that Neil might be the only man on the trip but there were several others there, too. There were about twenty of us altogether. All ages, from young to old, married and unmarried, and we all had a wonderful time. I made several new friends and we exchanged addresses.

'Our trip to Donegal started on a Sunday and we spent most of the day travelling. Tours were arranged to various places like Daniel's school, his church and his home and the Cope. And then we went further afield to visit the wider area of Donegal. On our first morning, as we got on the coach there was a film crew arriving to do a film about Daniel and they asked if they could join us on the coach to do some filming. We ended up in Kincasslagh Hall singing Danny Boy three times and they interviewed various members of our party before leaving us.

'Later in the afternoon when we arrived back at the Viking House, Daniel was in the bar being interviewed and he came out to greet us. There was a lot of clamouring for photos. I just stood quietly with my husband when Daniel asked me if I was on the tour. I said, "Yes," and he came across and had a chat with Neil and I before giving me a kiss and shaking Neil's hand. I didn't realize it but the film crew had been filming this and they asked if we could have the kiss again for the cameras. As you might imagine, I went weak at the knees but in the interest of television journalism I forced myself to repeat the exercise.

'We met Daniel later that night when he came back to the hotel to sign autographs and pictures and to pose for photographs. The following night Daniel came to the Viking House again and spent some more time singing and dancing and cracking jokes. At one stage he was up dancing on the table right in front of us, pretending he was going to swing from the chandeliers. Even my husband agreed that he'd had a wonderful time. He's very patient and quietly puts up with my obsession, although I do hear him walking

the fans' special day is like a cross between a church fete and a pilgrimage to lourdes.

around the house whistling Daniel tunes sometimes.'

Many Daniel O'Donnell fans are undoubtedly drawn to his music by way of O'Donnell's magnetic and engaging personality. The community of fandom that surrounds Daniel can be very enticing and Daniel's concerts work as reunions for hundreds of fans who only meet up on Daniel business. But there are also those who appreciate him as an artist first and foremost. Gill from Lewes has been a country music fan for many years and feels that people forget sometimes just how good Daniel is on stage. 'What annoys me is that people, and I don't really mean the fans but the press and the media, always talk about how Daniel has all these middle-aged female fans and how he's sold over ten million records and over a million videos and all these kinds of things. They seem to overlook the fact that he is a wonderful singer. His voice is quite exceptional and the songs suit him perfectly. You have no doubt that he means every word he sings. I've been to a few shows though I must admit I'm not as devoted as some of his fans but his concerts are among the best I have ever seen. Everybody feels a part of the show.'

Daniel with the people, where he belongs.

chapter

in my darkest hour

up to 1991, everything in daniel's

career had gone smoothly and he

was a household name in ireland

and the uk.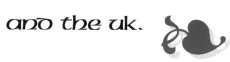

Happy Years. The troubled times over, Daniel can smile again.

He'd met some of his musical heroes such as Charley Pride and Loretta Lynn. He'd had his own national TV show in Ireland, with guest appearances by Lorrie Morgan and Stella Parton from the US as well as top Irish acts such as Mary Duff, Susan McCann, The Dubliners and Foster and Allen.

Then there was his recording trip to Nashville, appearances on American TV and his live performance at the Grand Ole Opry. He could sell out a concert tour in hours rather than days and the albums and videos were selling by the million. But in December 1991 the downside of success reared its ugly head. Daniel was exhausted. For the first time in his career he had to cancel a show. At one performance, which he manfully attempted to force himself through, he felt so weak he had to tell the audience he wasn't sure how long his voice would hold out. Finally, no manner of forcing himself could escape the inevitable conclusion that Daniel had lost his voice and would not be able to perform. He saw a throat specialist but still felt generally unwell. A herbalist finally fixed the problem by diagnosing Daniel as having an out-of-position diaphragm. With manipulation and herbal treatments, O'Donnell was finally able to recuperate and fight his way back to full strength. In retrospect, the enforced retirement had a positive effect on Daniel. He turned to God during his darkest hours and began taking a more active interest in religion and, eventually, gospel music. It also made him realize how his career could so easily be taken from him and after his return he seemed even more determined to make the most of every moment. Moreover, the time away allowed manager Sean Reilly to plan a large scale comeback show at The Point in Dublin. The Point is one of the largest venues in Ireland and is usually home to international rock and pop figures, not a homegrown country singer. But promoter Kieran Cavanagh reckoned he could sell enough tickets and the 6000 needed to fill the hall dutifully turned up to see Daniel back at his best.

Since then, Daniel O'Donnell has entered a more mature, more

Daniel enjoys a joke with celebrity and number one fan, Father Brian D'Arcy.

considered phase of his career. Without upsetting his fans, he has managed to limit some of his public commitments simply by managing his time better and planning events such as the annual open day rather than making himself available to his public 24 hours a day, seven days a week, as he did before the setback. And the past five years have seen Daniel O'Donnell consolidate himself as Ireland's answer to Garth Brooks. Concerts sell out swiftly and he has one of the best run and most devoted fan clubs in the pop business.

He has become a familiar face on national TV shows such as *GMTV*, *The Big Breakfast*, *Saturday Special* and *Songs Of Praise* and performs with easy grace. He is a natural with the TV chat show format and his 1997 appearance on the popular *Mrs Merton* comedy show was an undoubted success. Essentially, the show is played for laughs since Mrs Merton, practically a blue rinse stereotype of the older Daniel fan, is in fact thirtysomething comedienne Caroline Aherne. Her audience of senior citizens is largely a send-up and many guests without the ability to laugh at themselves have suffered at her hands. Daniel, of course, was in his element, playing the game effortlessly and spotting women in the audience to charm just as he does during his concert shows.

The years of hard work playing the country music circuit finally paid off in 1997, when he was given a special award for services to country music by the British Country Music Awards panel in Birmingham, a show that was broadcast on national BBC television.

He has sold over fourteen million albums and the signs are that sales are still rising. His last show at Birmingham's NEC sold out the 12,000 tickets in less than one hour.

In 1996, Daniel visited Romania. He was so moved by the plight of children living in squalor that he decided to donate all the proceeds from his single 'Give A Little Love' to Romania's biggest orphanage because he suddenly realized that 'this is what those lyrics were written for. My sister was sure that I would return from Romania with two or three children and we have seriously considered it. We've got plenty of room, after all. But it's difficult what with being single,' he told *The Scotsman* in 1997.

Single he may be, but in 1998 Daniel set rumourmongers clucking by admitting he was in love. Scotland's *Daily Record* has long kept readers up to date on the activities of its favourite singing Irishman and last year it reported that Daniel was involved with a young lady called Rose. The pair appeared together at a beauty contest at Dungloe. According to the paper, there had been some controversy when Rose's ex-boyfriend reportedly threatened to scar her face if she didn't leave Daniel alone. Her family denied the story and it would appear that Daniel and his lady are very much an item. Rose spent a week with Daniel and his family in Kincasslagh and recently accompanied him on his Australian tour. Daniel stated: 'If I was Johnny from down the road nobody would be interested in this situation. I would like to be Johnny down the road. We want to be left alone and have as normal a relationship as we

here's to you, daniel

' *I have to admit that I've never been a fan of his music, but I've always believed that, until somebody was successful in Britain at selling country music, then it would always be second rate compared to America. I think that Daniel O'Donnell has shown that there is a future for country music in Europe and that a non-American can indeed have a career in the States.* '

Alan Cackett – country music writer

Daniel with fellow star Gay Byrne.

can. We like each other and who knows what the future holds?'

But Daniel O'Donnell will never be a normal Joe. His legions of fans, and all those who take a casual interest in his career and music, would never allow that to happen. Daniel really wouldn't want it, anyway. He has worked hard for his success, honing his craft and spending time in the company of his admirers. For many it would turn their heads, but Daniel O'Donnell genuinely seems as unaffected by stardom, money and success as anyone in showbusiness could possibly be.

When Daniel O'Donnell finally appeared in public with a girlfriend it finally put paid to the gossip and speculation which is directed at any unmarried pop star in their mid-thirties. As with every aspect of his life, Daniel has refused to bow to pressure to conform and settle down just for the sake of his image. In interviews he has admitted to a certain sadness about not having a special person in his life, but he has found so little time for genuine romance, such has been his devotion and commitment to both his career and his fans.

In *Follow Your Dream*, Daniel talks of a female best friend, Josephine, but

he is a natural with the tv chat

show format and his 1997

appearance on the popular mrs

merton comedy show was an

undoubted success.

their relationship has only ever been platonic. He also refers to a young woman with whom he had a relationship in the 1980s, but he refuses to go into detail. 'I think if I revealed any of the intimate details of any of my relationships, it would be a betrayal,' he wrote.

Obviously, career obligations have kept Daniel from true love, so it was fitting that he should meet his first great love, Rose, through his work. They are, at the time of writing, inseparable. Fittingly, if any artist were to marry one of his fans, it should be the boy from Donegal, Daniel O'Donnell.

The 1998 tours of Australia and the United States continued the trend for playing larger and more prestigious venues on every visit and in late 1998 a record business development left Daniel looking even more secure as a recording artist than he had done in the previous ten years. Ritz Records bought independent label and distribution outfit Grapevine, home of artists like Mary Black and Emmylou Harris, in an attempt to widen its marketing and distribution base. With new resources and a wider distribution network, the signs were that Daniel O'Donnell's 1998 album, *Love Songs*, would be his most successful to date. ❧

chapter

who is daniel o'donnell?

this is a compilation of my conversations and interviews with daniel and, as befits his domination of the uk country music charts over the past decade, it's in the shape of a top 20.

Once the star could only stare, awe-struck, at Cliff Richard.

How important is America in your career?

'I first went there on a holiday when I was young and it was a real thrill to see all the things you know from television and the movies. It's a wonderful country and I've often taken my holidays there. Nashville was great, of course, because it's such a special place in country music. At first, I expected to see more going on there, but once I realized how Nashville was I had a great time. It's very easygoing and to play at the Grand Ole Opry was a very special moment.

'Branson is a nice place, too, and I've met some interesting and some very nice people over there. It would be nice to play more shows there and I think that's something that will happen with time. I think one of the greatest pleasures I've found in Americans is the differences in the language. I've got myself into trouble, I can tell you, on a few occasions. And the people there do have trouble understanding the way I talk. It's all part of what travelling is about. I'm always thinking about my next US trip.'

Who are your musical heroes?

'I have absolute admiration for Sir Cliff Richard. I was totally in awe the first time I met him. I admire his singing, of course, but also the way he has handled himself over the years. He sets a very good example. From country music, I have been lucky enough to meet two of my great heroes, Charley Pride and Loretta Lynn. Loretta Lynn is my favourite singer of all time. I even went to her home and did the tour. When she appeared on my TV show, it was very special. I was a nervous wreck. I didn't know how I was going to actually meet her. When I finally did, she was so beautiful and so pleasant that she put me at ease, but inside I was still shaking. And that's not really like me. Usually, I'm a very calm, unflappable kind of a person. But she is incredible. She came from very poor beginnings, had her first child at fourteen and still became a star and wrote her own songs. And she's still an amazing singer today. She is very special.'

How do you feel about the devotion of your fans?

'To start with, I am no different to them. I did with Loretta Lynn exactly what fans do with me. I was completely overawed and didn't dare speak. Before I met her, I had visited her home just like my fans do with me. I'm a fan, too. I think some performers place themselves above the audience. I have never done that. I love meeting people. It's the way I am. Meeting new people is one of the pleasures in life. I feel humbled by the fans; I certainly don't feel worthy of their affection, but I do appreciate it very much. I don't necessarily like the word "fan". To me, they are friends and some I know better than others. A lot of people who come to the shows are like family and friends now. It's not my duty to spend time with them, it's my pleasure.'

Are you nervous before a big show?

'Funnily enough, the scale of the concert doesn't really affect me. I'm always a little bit nervous, I suppose, but I'm probably much more nervous doing interviews and doing chat shows and things like that than I am about going on stage. I prepare very well and I feel very comfortable getting up on stage and entertaining people. It's what I do best, so I've become pretty confident. And I love it. That time on stage is what it's all about really.'

You have been criticized a great deal by the press. Does it hurt?

Nobody likes to be criticized, obviously. Even as a child I was picked on because I wasn't like all the others. I've always been mild and gentle, I suppose, and for some reason some people really don't like that. The criticism started in my career, I think, because I was young and I was singing an older style of music than many people my age would have performed. But that's what I'm like. I really can't see what the problem is. I can only be myself and I think that the people who know me would say that I am an honest person.'

How would you describe your music?

'I sing all kinds of music – old songs, new songs. I grew up on Irish music and country music and now I think there's a nice balance. If I like a song I want to sing it – it doesn't matter to me what style it is. I think people were surprised a while back when I did Elvis songs in my show. At the end of the day, if it seems right I want to sing it. Most recently I've been looking towards gospel music. I'm not sure where that will lead.'

How do you remember your childhood?

'It was good. I was a happy child and I remember those days very fondly. It was hard in many ways. My father died when I was young but I don't feel that

here's to you, Daniel

'I booked him for the Theatre Royal in Norwich because I'd read about his success and I personally liked the music. It was a departure for us and a little risky for him and his people, but I was not surprised to see the terrific response the first time he played for us. And he conducted himself so courteously that the whole show was very smooth and easy for us to work with.'

Dick Condon – theatre manager

I suffered. I had a great family and my mother was amazing. Growing up in Donegal was a wonderful time. People love to dabble in pop psychology and tell me that my loss must mean this or that but, really, I think I coped very well, and so did the rest of my family.'

How do you cope with the constant travelling?

'It gets tiring sometimes, but I've been on the road for a long time. It becomes routine. I remember that when I wasn't touring, when I had my voice problem, it felt really strange to be getting up early in the morning because I had become so used to late nights and getting up at lunch time. It becomes part of your life. Obviously, these days the travelling is much more comfortable than when I started out. And I have all my friends with me and we'll get to the hotel and there will be fans there already. It's really a very nice thing.'

Are you still developing as an artist?

'I hope so. I think you have to improve with experience. I'm always thinking about the show and what we might do. I watch other people, like Sir Cliff, and take mental notes. I learned a lot from Margo, my sister, in the early days and I would hate to think that I couldn't continue to improve as a performer.'

How important was your sister in the beginning of your career?

Margo encouraged me but most importantly she set me an example. I understood what it meant to be a singer and I always knew that it involved lots of travelling and doing interviews and meeting people. She kind of paved the way for me. I think I would have found things harder if I hadn't had a sister who had already been successful in the music industry.'

How do you think you music will progress?

'I've become very interested in gospel music recently. I really enjoy that and certainly want to pursue that style. It's a great feeling to perform gospel and, while it may be slightly different to some of the usual material, I feel very happy with it. I've always enjoyed doing *Songs Of Praise* and definitely want to devote more time to that side of my career.

You seem to be surrounded by people who you trust and who have treated you well.

'I've been very lucky. My manager Sean Reilly is a very good man and we have worked together for a long time now. We discuss everything and it works well. My record company are like a family, really, and I owe a great deal to everyone there and especially Mick Clerkin. And then there's the fan club. So many people put so much time and energy into making the Daniel O'Donnell career work smoothly. I couldn't have done it without them.'

Do you feel a special bond with Ritz Records?

'It's been like my second family for a long time now. They are more than friends and I truly respect the other artists on the label as well. Some have been more successful than others, but I've admired all the different artists that Ritz have worked with. Having Mary Duff on tour is something very special, too. I think we are very good friends and her musical style is perfectly suited to the shows we do together. I cannot imagine my career in any other way. And I owe Mr Clerkin a lot. He saw potential in me when I was very raw and all the other record labels I approached thought I lacked what it needed to make it in this business

Are you as comfortable doing television shows as you are on stage?

'No. My own television shows were good to do but there is so much to think about. On stage I know exactly what is going on. With television there's a whole team of people controlling things. I'm not very comfortable with being interviewed on chat shows, because I don't really enjoy talking about myself, but the ones I've done have all gone fairly well, I think.'

How deeply were you affected by what you saw in Romania?

'It was heartbreaking. All these orphan children living in very bad conditions. That's why I got involved with the charity single to raise money for a halfway house for them. It's very upsetting to see people suffer, especially children.

Hopefully I can do some good and help raise some money for them.'

How do you feel about the Daniel O'Donnell jokes?

'It's a strange thing, you know, to have people tell jokes about you. They've become quite famous. Journalists always find them and put them in articles about me. As most of the fans know I like to laugh and if the joke is funny I'll laugh, too. I know how my image is and the media always exaggerates everything. I like a good joke, even if it is at my expense.'

Is it true that your father was a healer?

'Well, evidently he did have a healing ability. He was the seventh son of a seventh son and that is supposed to give a person special gifts. I was young when he died, of course, but I've heard stories from my family how he could help heal neighbours and things like that. I know what you're coming to, because some people have suggested that my concerts are something like a healer's revival meeting in America. I meet lots of sick people in my work and I'm always kind, but I don't believe I have any special powers.'

Do you still remember the first time you actually played the Grand Ole Opry?

'Oh, I'll remember that for the rest of my life. George Hamilton made things easy with the arrangements and just concentrated on making me feel at ease. I don't usually get very nervous, but when you go there you literally feel the history and I was privileged and honoured and very scared.'

Are there any ambitions left?

'Oh, I don't know. I tend to take each step as it comes. I have people who think ahead for me so I can concentrate on the job at hand. Obviously, I want to continue what we've achieved internationally, but right now I feel my heart moving towards gospel music. That has become very important for me.'

To what do you attribute you phenomenal success?

'That's easy. Lots of luck, lots of hard work and finding the right people along the way.'

Danny Boy – a personal view

As I stated at the beginning of this book, Daniel O'Donnell is a pop music phenomenon and, hopefully, what you have just read goes some to explaining why that is so.

Danny Boy – the ultimate entertainer.

As is so often the case with a phenomenon, the human aspect of the individual involved is more difficult to grasp. Daniel O'Donnell does not make it easy to get close to the man inside, the emotional side of the musical phenomenon. He doesn't wear his heart on his sleeve. Indeed, the seemingly easy-going charmer from Donegal is, in fact, a complex character who has either refused or deftly avoided analysis by the many writers who have tried to understand and/or explode the 'Mr Nice Guy' image.

He spends endless hours chatting with friends and strangers, both during his working life and his time at home, yet finds answering questions about his life, his childhood and his own psyche painfully difficult. The avoidance is possibly a defensive reaction to the countless attempts to 'blow his cover' and find something supposedly more sinister behind the facade.

It's possibly a sad indictment of the times we live in, that the fact that even today Daniel spends a great amount of time with his mother is looked upon suspiciously. She lives in his bungalow in Kincasslagh and plays a major part in his career by supporting fully all the fan-related activities and proudly receiving the hordes of Daniel followers who make the pilgrimage to Donegal. Daniel has said many times that he owes his mother a great deal for setting him on the path to success, by instilling the right values and being a constant source of support throughout the highs and few lows of his career. Because Daniel O'Donnell is very much his own man, he has ensured his mother lives in comfort and has never been ashamed to be known as a pop star who, in his mid 30s, still lives with his mother.

From an early age, Daniel O'Donnell was a target for older boys as well as his peers, who teased the more gentle-minded and sensitive Daniel for refusing to swear, fight and roughhouse like them. He was regarded as a 'mammy's boy' from an early age and that stigma has stuck throughout his career. Obviously, his father's death when Daniel was just six played a major part in his spending a larger percentage of time with his mother than might have been expected. Watching Daniel now, and talking with those who know him best, it seems he's never happier and more contented than when leaning over the garden fence for a good old natter with an older woman. Having spent so much time in the company of older women, he relates naturally to their conversations and responds with empathy and, apparently, great understanding. That his audience is to a large extent made up of middle-aged women is hardly surprising. These are the people to whom he relates on a most natural level.

The intensity with which some people have decided to dislike Daniel, his image and his success must seem remarkably familiar to Daniel and is easily

equated with the bullying he suffered as a child. The many – often cruel – Daniel O'Donnell jokes are a case in point. For example: 'The IRA capture Tony Blair, Ian Paisley and Daniel O'Donnell. They only have two bullets. Who do they shoot? Daniel O'Donnell, twice, just to make sure.'

Despite the edge to the jokes, Daniel has said that, while he finds it mystifying that people should invent jokes about him, he does find some of them funny. An ability to laugh at oneself is a rare gift and also a precious, defensive one – making jokes about oneself never hurts as much as if another gets there first. Which is a lesson that countless comedians and entertainers over the years have learned and revealed about themselves.

Another, common child's reaction to bullying or robust teasing is to withdraw, to guard against further attack. A child who has suffered the kind of teasing which Daniel appears to have suffered in Donegal understands inherently that knowledge is power and that to give away information about themselves is to provide ammunition for their tormentors. As an adult, this knowledge is more certain, which can explain why Daniel is so cautious about revealing too much of his inner self to the prying press. In a one-on-one situation with friends and fans he's natural and easy, but in front of strangers who are attempting to put him on the spot reticence is the order of the day. He's acutely aware that there are people waiting gleefully to destroy his persona.

Daniel's reticence has also been a key part of his success. He is a shrewd businessman who has slowly but surely consolidated his position in popular music. Daniel would most likely argue that it takes strength of character to remain an outsider, to refuse to join the gang and follow his own path. That stubborn streak was honed early in his life as he refused to be pressured by his peers, and it was later sharpened by his determined first attempts at forging a career in music.

The supposed squeaky clean 'mammy's boy' is, in fact, a single-minded and very resolute person who has always worked to the beat of his own

drum. He has taken few risks and, while never afraid to try new things, he definitely understands the nature of his fan base. There is no hint of Daniel being a frustrated artist forced to play music that only pleases his fans. O'Donnell loves his romantic-nostalgic material as much as the older audiences who pay to see him. There has been no fabled music business contrivance, no manipulation by a Svengali-like manager. In some ways, Daniel O'Donnell was always old before his time. He has always enjoyed the company and the pleasures of those more advanced in years than himself. How his career will develop over the next ten years or so remains to be seen, but for the moment, Daniel O'Donnell will continue to give away the bare essentials to the media, while at the same time giving as much of himself as he possibly can to the people who really do matter to him; the fans.

here's to you, daniel

'*I love the music and I know Daniel pretty well, I
think. But what makes going on his tours so
special is the community feeling that everyone
has. It's like a party with old friends every night
and with the added bonus of a great show at the
end of it. There's a lot of energy among the fans.
They really have a good time at Daniel concerts
and I think that one day people will realize just
what a phenomenon he has been.*'

Frank Mckenna – Irish fan

Discography

The Two Sides of Daniel O'Donnell   **Ritz 1985**

The Green Glens Of Antrim/The Blue Hills Of Breffni/Any Tipperary Town/The Latchyco/Home Town On The Foyle/These Are My Mountains/My Donegal Shore/Crying My Heart Out Over You/My Old Pal/Our House Is A Home/Your Old Love Letters/21 Years/Highway 40 Blues/I Wouldn't Change You If I Could

I Need You   **Ritz 1986**

I Need You/Sing An Old Irish Song/From A Jack To A King/Lovely Rose Of Clare/Stand Beside Me/Irish Eyes/Dear Old Galway Town/Three Leaf Shamrock/Veil Of White Lace/Kickin' Each Other's Hearts Around/Medals For Mothers/Wedding Bells/Snowflake/Your Friendly Irish Way/Lough Melvin's Rocky Shore/I Love You Because

From The Heart   **Telstar 1988**

The Minute You're Gone/It Doesn't Matter Anymore/Mary From Dungloe/Bye Bye Love/The Old Rugged Cross/Wasting My Time/Kelly/Things/Act Naturally/Honey/Wooden Heart/It Keeps Right On A'Hurtin'/My Bonnie Maureen/I Know That You Know/Old Dungarvan Oak/Danny Boy

Thoughts From Home   **Telstar 1989**

My Shoes Keep Walking Back To You/Mountains Of Mourne/London Leaves/Blue Eyes Crying In The Rain/Old Days Remembered/Send Me The Pillow You Dream On/Moonlight And Roses/A Little Piece Of Heaven/Far Far From Home/Isle Of Innisfree/My Heart Skips A Beat/I Know One/I'll Take You Home Again Kathleen/Second Fiddle/My Favourite Memory/Forty Shades Of Green

Favourites   **Ritz 1990**

Bed Of Roses/Forever You'll Be MIne/Excuse Me (I Think I've Got A Heartache)/Halo Of Gold/The Streets Of Baltimore/Geisha Girl/Life To Go/That's A Sad Affair/Bringing Mary Home/Home Sweet Home/The Banks Of My Own Lovely Lee/Home Is Where The Heart Is/Dublin In The Rare Ould Times/The Green Hills Of Sligo

The Last Waltz   **Ritz 1990**

Here I Am In Love Again/We Could/Last Waltz Of The Evening/When Only The Sky Was Blue/Heaven With You/You Know I Still Love You/Talk Back Trembling Lips/The Shelter Of Your Eyes/When We Get Together/Ring Of Gold/A Fool Such As I/Memory Number One/Look Both Ways/Little Patch Of Blue/Marianne

Follow Your Dream   **Ritz 1991**

Follow Your Dream/Welcome Home/Back In My Baby's Arms Again/Not Until The Next Time/My Claim To Fame Is You/Sweet Memories/I Just Want To Dance With You/Sweet Memories/The Love In Your Eyes/You're The Reason/Belle Of The Ball/Galway Bay/Destination Donegal/How Great Thou Art

The Very Best Of   **Ritz 1991**

I Need You/Never Ending Song Of Love/Don't Forget To Remember/A Country Boy Like Me/She's No Angel/Stand Beside Me/Eileen/Pretty Little Girl From Omagh/Danny Boy/The Wedding Song/My Donegal Shore/Letter From The Postman's Bag/The Three Bells/Our House Is A Home/A Loved One's Goodbye/Home Is Where The Heart is/The Old Rugged Cross/You Send Me Your Love/Take Good Care Of Her/Standing Room Only

Discography

Especially For You **Ritz 1994**
Singing The Blues/Leaving Is Easy When Loving Is Hard/She Goes Walking Through My Mind/Happy Years /Broken Hearts Always Mend/Guilty/Travelling Light/Come Back Paddy Reilly To Ballyjamesduff/Whatever Happened To Old/Fashioned Love/Sweet Forget Me Not/You're The First Thing I Think Of/It Comes And Goes/Silver Threads Among The Gold/Someday You'll Want Me To Want You/Lovers Chain/Never Be Anyone Else But You

Timeless (With Mary Duff) **Ritz 1996**
Timeless/We Believe In Happy Endings/I Won't Take Less Than Your Love/Whispering Hope/Have You Ever Been Lonely/I Heard The Bluebird Sing/Eileen McManus /Secret Love/Vaya Con Dios/Walk Right Back/Just Someone I Used To Know/Jeannie's Afraid Of The Dark/Somewhere Between/Will The Circle Be Unbroken

Songs of Inspiration **Ritz 1996**
Footsteps/It Is No Secret/You Needed Me/I Saw The Light/One Day At A Time/My Forever Friend/What A Friend We Have In Jesus/Why Me Lord/The Old Rugged Cross/Yes, I Really Love You/How Great Thou Art /This World Is Not My Home /He Took My Place/Amazing Grace/Family Bible/In The Garden/Children's Band/Standing Room Only

Love Songs **Ritz 1998**
Save The Last Dance For Me/I Can't Stop Loving You/You're The Only Good Thing (That's Happened To Me)/Limerick You're A Lady

US RELEASES:

Country Collection **Honest/Ritz 1997**
The Shelter Of Your Eyes/I Know One/She Goes Walking Through My Mind/Bye Bye Love/Blue Eyes Cryin' In The Rain/Sweet Memories/Guilty/Leaving Is Easy (When Loving Is Hard)/We Could/Silver Threads Among The Gold/Cryin' Time/The Last Waltz Of The Evening

Irish Collection **Honest/Ritz 1997**
Sing An Old Irish Song/My Donegal Shore/Pretty Little Girl From Omagh/Pat Murphy's Meadow/Green Glens Of Antrim/I'll Take You Home Again Kathleen/Forty Shades Of Green/Dublin In The Rare Ould Times/The Isle Of Innisfree/Irish Eyes/Galway Bay/The Old Dungarvan Oak/The Mountains Of Mourne/Any Tipperary Town

This is Daniel O'Donnell
Moonlight And Roses/I Just Want To Dance With You/Danny Boy/Roses Are Red(My Love)/Never Be Anyone Else But You/The Wedding/Someday You'll Want Me To Want You/Marianne/The Love In Your Eyes/You're The Reason/The Three Bells/How Great Thou Art

picture credits

The Irish Times . . . . **pages 103, 106**

Mirror Syndication . . . . **pages 25, 26, 68, 95, 120**

Photocall . . . . **pages 53, 59, 71**

Redferns . . . . **pages 10, 20, 36, 49, 60, 77, 85, 117, 122, 124, 128**

Rex . . . . **pages 13, 42, 44, 47, 65, 83, 88, 92, 113**

Scope . . . . **pages 3, 7, 15, 29, 31, 55, 67, 73, 87, 99, 101, 105, 109, 111, 119**

Bibliography

Follow Your Dream
by Daniel O'Donnell with Eddie Rowley *(O'Brien Press 1992)*

The World of Country Music
by Andrew Vaughan *(St Martin's Press 1992)*

Publications

Country Music International, Country Music Round-Up, **Country Muisc People**, Country Gazette, **Country Weekly**, Billboard, **Music Week**, Daily Record, **Irish Independent**, Irish Times, **Sunday Telegraph**, Sunday World, **Hot Press**